THE TEACHING OF LATIN
IN AMERICAN SCHOOLS

THE TEACHING OF LATIN
IN AMERICAN SCHOOLS:
A Profession in Crisis

RICHARD A. LaFLEUR
Editor

SCHOLARS PRESS

Published Under the Auspices of the American Classical League
and the American Philological Association
With the Support of the National Endowment for the Humanities

THE TEACHING OF LATIN
IN AMERICAN SCHOOLS

Richard A. LaFleur
Editor

©1987
American Classical League
and the American Philological Association

Library of Congress Cataloging in Publication Data

The Teaching of Latin in American schools.

1. Latin philology--Study and teaching--United States.
2. Latin philology--Teacher training--United States.
3. Civilization, Classical--Study and teaching--United
States. I. LaFleur, Richard A. II. American Philological
Association. III. American Classical League.
PA2065.U5T43 1987   478'.007'073   87-12678
ISBN 1-55540-150-3

Printed in the United States of America
on acid-free paper

To the Teachers of Latin in America's Schools—
Yesterday's, Today's . . . and Tomorrow's

Table of Contents

Preface

In the seven years since the publication of the Lyman Report (Commission, reference no. 1, below), there has been serious and fruitful debate about the place of the Humanities in American schools. After the extremes of the late 1960s, during which it was fashionable to advocate the dismantling of recognizable structures in many areas of education, the pendulum swung towards the sometimes equally pernicious doctrines of the so-called "Back to Basics" movement. It is small wonder that in the decade before the Lyman Report teachers, parents, and students were confused. For the Humanities the 1970s were years of lost opportunity, in which the forces of anti-intellectualism—always a strong presence in American history (Hofstadter, ref. no. 2)—and the cowardice of those who feared the notion of a disciplined education combined to inflict great damage. Yet throughout these same dark years there were many thoughtful people, especially among teachers at all levels inside and beyond the Humanities, who saw in the confusion a way of preserving, yet transforming, the place of the Humanities in a democratic system of education. Among these leaders—for an active concern with the proper balance of education is truly a form of leadership—have been many teachers of the Classics in schools and universities, whose work is the basis of the challenges presented by this book.

The book's subtitle, *A Profession in Crisis*, only tells part of the story. Out of the crisis of the Classics has come new thinking about the place of the ancient languages and civilizations, which in its turn has led to many positive developments in educational planning, research, and, above all, teaching. The reader will immediately be struck by the sheer variety of problems and answers, in itself proof of the vitality of the profession. It has been a profession suffering through the painful dilemmas of self-definition, but a profession whose members have no doubt of the justice of their claim to a fundamental place in American education. In this they have been ahead of many of their colleagues in other disciplines in the Humanities, many of whom could learn much from the programs—often exciting and ingenious, always planned with intellectual integrity—that are described in the narrative parts of this book.

The basic dilemma facing the Classics profession has been how to define its goals, and consequently the scope of its teaching.

Traditionally, as the title of the book shows, the goals have been
limited to the ancient languages (in practice this has meant one
ancient language in most cases), and the mental disciplines of the
subject have been those inculcated by the rigors of philology. This
is still the foundation of our discipline, yet it is no longer the whole
of it. The expectations of students and parents now extend to the
teaching of other aspects of the ancient world, and it is in adjusting
to these demands that our profession has faced a crisis. In the first
place, neither the traditional training of teachers nor the existing
programs in schools have been flexible enough to meet the need
for systematic teaching of the ancient civilizations and their
history. Secondly, the training and supply of teachers in the
languages—that is, in the very foundation of our discipline—have
for at least 20 years been in a decline, as can be seen from the stark
accounts given in the reports in this book. I believe that the
profession has faced the problems of definition and of the supply of
professional teachers with courage and honesty, and also with long
debate and many painful decisions. This is perhaps the most
important message in this collection of essays: classicists have
thought maturely about their place in American education in the
last quarter of the twentieth century, and they have developed
solutions to problems that 10 years ago seemed overwhelming.

Now, we must ask, is anyone paying attention? Here there are
grounds for optimism. In the first place, it is a fact that the federal
government has given strong support to efforts at achieving the
goals that classicists have defined. The reader will immediately be
struck by the frequency with which the National Endowment for
the Humanities (NEH) is mentioned throughout the book. Especially since the publication of the Lyman Report, the NEH has
challenged teachers and administrators to develop appropriate
programs: one could mention the Summer Seminars and Institutes
for Teachers, or the encouragement given to cooperative programs,
on a local, institutional, or regional basis, between universities and
schools. These are but a few examples from many. Equally
important has been the readiness of the profession to develop its
own answers to the challenges using available resources, with a
variety and ingenuity that must impress even the most superficial
readers of this volume. These challenges have brought changes,
many of them welcome, still more of them necessary. Besides the
new definitions of the goals of our profession, we have come to
think more flexibly about the range of our teaching: programs in
Latin and the classical literatures in translation have broken new
ground in elementary-school teaching, to give one example, and, at
the other end of the spectrum, there have been a number of new

programs in which universities are cooperating with teachers in the schools in a partnership that is long overdue. Indeed, this proper sense of collegiality among teachers at all levels, from elementary through university, is one of the most heartening results flowing from the crisis of the profession.

And here, perhaps, is an important reason for optimism. A recent conference on "The Classics in American Schools" was funded by the National Endowment for the Humanities with a grant made to the American Philological Association (APA). The APA, whose traditional focus has been upon scholarly research in the Classics, joined with the American Classical League (ACL), whose focus is primarily upon the teaching of the Classics in schools, to organize the conference. Its report is being edited by a past president of the ACL, and participants were teachers and administrators in schools, universities, and professional associations, drawn not only from the Classics but from many other disciplines and professions. Surely this is a paradigm for the future. Readers of this book will for a short time only be alarmed by the crisis that it documents. For far longer they will be encouraged by the answers that professional classicists have already given, and they will be challenged themselves to join with their colleagues in seeing that the languages and civilizations of the ancient world take their rightful place in a modern and democratic education.

Mark Morford
University of Virginia
December 1986

REFERENCES

1. Commission on the Humanities. *The Humanities in America.* Berkeley, CA: Univ. of California Press, 1980.

2. Hofstadter, Richard. *Anti-intellectualism in American Life.* New York, NY: Knopf, 1964.

Introduction

In 1962 there were more than 700,000 students enrolled in Latin classes in America's public secondary schools. By 1976 the number had plummeted nearly 80% to only about 150,000. College Latin dropped at the same time, though not quite so precipitously, from approximately 40,000 in 1965 to fewer than 25,000 in 1974. The causes of the decline were many and complex, but they certainly all related in one way or another to the upheaval that shook our society throughout the 1960s and into the mid-1970s. Traditional institutions were challenged, besieged, and in some instances ravaged, not least the curricula of our schools and colleges. Interest and enrollments in even the modern languages were eroded during this period, as high-school administrators and counselors took their signal from colleges and universities, the vast majority of which were dropping language requirements for both admission and graduation. But naturally it was Latin, that unloved relic from the past ("first it killed the Romans, and now it's killing me . . ."), which suffered the most damaging assault during that decade and a half of Relevancies and Cafeteria-line Curricula. Along with enrollments, participation in national examinations such as the College Board's Latin Achievement Test (AT) and the Advanced Placement (AP) Exam, and memberships in local and national classical associations declined sharply: National Junior Classical League (NJCL) memberships, for example, fell from about 107,000 in 1964 to less than 29,000 a decade later. To many during this period—not least those who might have considered teaching Latin as a profession or those teachers who might have encouraged their students' interests in that direction—it appeared that Latin was indeed on its way to becoming a dead language.

Since 1976, of course, the situation has been dramatically reversed, owing to a complex of factors considered in some detail in this volume's opening essay and including the "Back to Basics" movement, the recommendations of the Carter Commission and other national education study groups of the past several years, the publication of research that demonstrated the significant positive correlation between studying Latin and improving English verbal skills, and the vigorous promotional efforts of such professional organizations as the American Classical League (ACL, which led the way in this regard), the American Philological Association (APA), the Classical Association of the Middle West and South

(CAMWS), and others. The resurgence of Latin became a favorite topic with the popular media beginning in the late 1970s: heralded by a November 12, 1979, *Newsweek* article, "The Return of the Classics," in which the possibility of a teacher shortage was perceptively forecast, the subject has remained in the local and national news since then, with dozens of feature stories in *Time, U.S. News and World Report*, the *New York Times*, the *Washington Post*, the *Wall Street Journal*, and, most recently, in a March, 1986, *Newsweek on Campus* feature (auspiciously titled, "Classical Renaissance: Getting a Solid Education—and Maybe Even a Job"), a September, 1986, *Christian Science Monitor* report ("Latin Redux"), and an Associated Press article by Dorothy Gast that appeared under a variety of titles in newspapers across the country during October and November, 1986.

In 1978 public high-school Latin enrollments rose, for the first time since 1962, to about 152,000, and by 1982 they had increased another 12.7%, to approximately 170,000. There is good reason to suppose, moreover, that the upward trend has continued steadily since 1982 (the latest year for which we currently have complete national figures: the next enrollment survey by the American Council on the Teaching of Foreign Languages [ACTFL], for 1985, will be published in *Foreign Language Annals* in the fall of 1987): across the country there remains a strong interest in establishing new Latin programs and revitalizing existing programs; livelier methods and materials for teaching Latin are being developed; NJCL memberships, up by more than 25% from the 1977 low of 29,000 to about 37,000 in 1982, rose another 33%, to nearly 50,000, in 1986; participation in the College Board's AT and AP exams continues to increase; and the number of participants in the ACL's National Latin Exam has grown steadily from approximately 9,000 in 1978 to over 33,000 in 1982 and 60,000 in 1986. The renaissance of Latin was a major focus of two independent national conferences in September, 1986, the Wethersfield Conference, "Latin in Today's World," sponsored by the Wethersfield Institute and held on the campus of Columbia University, and an APA/ACL-sponsored conference on "The Classics in American Schools," organized by APA Vice President Mark Morford, with funding from the National Endowment for the Humanities (NEH), and held on the grounds of the University of Virginia.

Thus we have succeeded over the past decade, and remarkably so, in generating "New Life for a Dead Language" (to borrow the title of a December 24, 1984, *Time* magazine feature essay) in secondary schools across the United States. Unhappily, according to surveys conducted by both the Modern Language Association

(MLA) and the ACL within the last three years, this growth in high-school Latin enrollments has not been matched in our colleges, and the number of Latin majors planning to teach the language has certainly not increased in proportion to the demand. Reports from national and regional Latin placement services and from the offices of state foreign language consultants across the country have indicated for the past several years that Latin teaching positions have markedly outnumbered available candidates. Predicted by some classicists as early as the late 1970s, the Latin teacher shortage we face today in most areas of the country has reached critical proportions.

As a consequence of this shortage, plans to open new Latin programs or to expand existing ones have again and again in recent years been curtailed or even abandoned. In numerous other instances, however, teachers lacking certification, or teachers certified in other areas but with some training in Latin—often only two or three courses, taken 10 or 20 years earlier, in college or even in high school—have been hired or reassigned to teach in these new or expanded programs; in cases too frequent to contemplate, teachers with no formal instruction in Latin at all are being sent into the classroom by desperate or overzealous principals. Under such circumstances—and the phenomenon is by no means limited, but is occurring in hundreds of classrooms and affecting thousands of high schoolers throughout America—the students, the teachers themselves, and ultimately the Classics profession as a whole will suffer. We dare not run the risk of creating a generation of poorly taught and uninspired Latin students.

This very critical teacher shortage, which has the potential to create enormous difficulties for the study of Classics in the United States, and for American education generally, has received increasing attention over the past few years. Again, the American Classical League has taken a leading role in this connection, under the presidencies of Professors Gilbert Lawall (1976-80), Mary Ann Burns (1980-84), and their successors, and through the work of the League's National Committee for Latin and Greek, whose members represent the constituencies of all major regional and national Classics professional associations. These organizations, especially CAMWS (through its Committee for the Promotion of Latin) and the APA (with Vice President Mark Morford chairing its Committee on Educational Services), together with a number of state and local classical associations as well as several individual university Classics departments, have now begun, along with ACL, to direct their energies toward alleviating the problem, identified as one of vital importance by Professor Helen North (Swarthmore College) in her 1984 APA report to the American Council of Learned Societies in support of the congressional re-authorization of the National Endowment for the Humanities. The Endowment itself has acknowledged the seriousness of the situation, generously supporting two national programs aimed at preparing bright but underqualified Latin teachers for certification, the Westminster Latin Institutes during 1984-85 and the ACL/University of Georgia (UGA) National Latin Institute during 1986-87 (both Institutes are described in detail in this volume).

The major thrust of my own term as ACL President (1984-86) was to confront the teacher shortage with every resource at my disposal, regarding the problem as far and away the single greatest crisis threatening the Classics profession in this decade. The ACL/UGA Latin Institute has been one product of that thrust: funded by an NEH grant of nearly $250,000, the Institute attracted more than 500 inquiries and 170 applications from teachers who for the most part fit the profile characterized above, teachers bright, able, and motivated, who had been appointed to Latin teaching positions within the past few years though they had only meager backgrounds in Latin and Roman culture. Other efforts of my office in the direction of alleviating the teacher shortage included: 1) researching and writing an article on trends in the study of Latin in American schools, which focused on enrollments in the secondary schools over the past two decades and on the current teacher shortage—published in the September, 1985, *Foreign Language Annals*, the study has been substantially updated and is included, with permission of ACTFL, as the opening essay in this volume; 2) requesting Robert Wilhelm (Miami University, Oxford, OH), in his capacity as Director of the ACL's Latin/Greek Teacher Placement Service, to conduct a thoroughgoing survey of the Latin placement situation across the country and to report his findings to the League—first published in the May/June, 1985, *Classical Outlook*, Professor Wilhelm's study has also been updated for this book, and to it has been added, as the closing item in the volume, a directory of state, regional, and national Latin placement services; 3) requesting that Professor Judith Sebesta (University of South Dakota), in her role as ACL Vice President and Program Chairman, arrange for the 1985 ACL Institute in Austin, Texas, a panel on the topic, "Meeting the Need for Latin Teachers"—revised versions of the papers presented on that panel, which underscored both the nature and scope of the teacher shortage and suggested several models for an effective response, are likewise included in this collection; 4) meeting with and addressing numerous professional groups around the country over the past three years, discussing the state of Latin in our secondary schools, articulating the challenges we face, and suggesting ways in which classicists in the schools and colleges might collaborate in responding to those challenges.

This book, funded by a grant from the National Endowment for the Humanities (Division of Education Programs) and by cost-sharing grants from the American Classical League, the American Philological Association, and the University of Georgia, represents the culmination of the efforts detailed above. In addition to this Introduction, and Professor Morford's Preface, the volume's contents include, first, two essays documenting the teacher shortage and providing an historical perspective on its development (the updated articles, mentioned earlier, from *Foreign Language Annals* and *Classical Outlook*, by myself and Professor Wilhelm); second, reports on the NEH-funded Westminster College and ACL/UGA National Latin Institutes, which are outlined here in considerable detail in order to serve as blueprints for comparable programs in the future; and, finally, ten other articles describing several different responses to the problems of Latin teacher training and (in the case of the last two papers) of Latin teacher placement developed by classicists and classical associations in various regions of the country, from New England, to Maryland and Virginia, to the deep South, to Texas and Colorado. As noted earlier, six of the papers derive originally from the 1985 ACL Institute panel, "Meeting the Need for Latin Teachers" (the essays by Castro, Keitel, Moreland and Schwartz, Davis and Mikalson, Kitchell, and King).

While the challenges we face in the Classics profession today are many and varied, as Professor Morford has remarked in his Preface, and range widely from the elementary classroom to the doctoral seminar, the most immediately critical of these challenges is surely the current and anticipated future shortage of qualified Latin teachers for the secondary schools. The purposes of this book are to document and underscore the seriousness of that shortage; to exhort college and university faculty to more vigorous and effective initiatives in assisting current, former, and prospective teachers toward acquiring certification in Latin; and to assist college departments in such efforts by describing a variety of effective teacher training and support programs. Each of the essays presents a unique perspective and set of experiences that should prove of considerable value to educators planning to undertake similar programs: while it is perhaps unlikely that the book will provide paradigms that can be replicated exactly by a particular department, inasmuch as both resources and temperaments will vary considerably from one institution or locale to another, it is nonetheless hoped that, taken as a whole, the essays in this collection will suggest models of action that, appropriately modified to suit local circumstances, might constructively advance the goals of the Classics profession. The volume is being distributed gratis to all Classics departments, all state foreign language consultants, and selected colleges of education, in each of the 50 states, with additional copies available to other educators and friends of the Classics who are disposed to support the profession's efforts at alleviating the teacher shortage. And with the volume comes a call to action.

Without question, the situation we face is a critical one, demanding a broad and intensive response on the part of classicists in the schools and colleges, language educators, and other professionals involved in educational decision-making. Much has been done within just the past two or three years, nationally and locally, to address the shortage and some of its troubling consequences. But still more must be done, both immediately and over the long term, if the matter is to be satisfactorily resolved and if our next generation of Latin students is to be not only more numerous, but also well trained themselves, appreciative of the quality of their high-school classroom experience, and enthusiastic not only to pursue their study of the Classics in our colleges and universities but also, some few of them at least, to enter the teaching profession. Some practical insights into what can be done—and what must be done—will be found, it may be hoped, in the pages of this book.

For their kind support of my work on this project and on related efforts at responding to the nation's shortage of Latin teachers, I am deeply indebted to very many persons, not all of whom can be named here; I am grateful, however, for the opportunity of expressing my thanks to the following: the very efficient and dedicated staff of the National Endowment for the Humanities, especially Stephanie Quinn Katz and Christine Kalke; the officers, staff, and membership of the American Classical League, for their unwavering confidence; the Board of Directors of the American Philological Association, most notably Mark Morford and George P. Goold; Professor Robert Rowland (University of Maryland), who generously offered to read and evaluate the manuscript on behalf of APA; officials of the Educational Testing Service, ACTFL, MLA, CAMWS, and the many other organizations that provided the data examined in my opening essay; the administration of the University of Georgia, in particular my Dean, Dr. William J. Payne, Academic Affairs Vice Presidents Virginia Y. Trotter and M.

Louise McBee, and Ronald D. Simpson and William K. Jackson, in our Office of Instructional Development; my colleagues in the Department of Classics, not least James C. Anderson, Jr., Assistant Director of our NEH Latin Institute; our Classics Department staff, including Mary Wells Ricks and Connie Russell, and especially JoAnn Pulliam, who typed the manuscript for the book; the book's contributors, for their enthusiastic cooperation and their patience; and my wife Laura, and our three children, for affectionately tolerating my alleged (and surely only occasional) single-mindedness.

Richard A. LaFleur
University of Georgia
December 1986

THE TEACHING OF LATIN IN AMERICAN SCHOOLS:
A Profession in Crisis

The Study of Latin in American Schools: Success and Crisis

Richard A. LaFleur
University of Georgia

The University of Georgia, chartered in 1785 and thus the nation's oldest state university, recently concluded its bicentennial celebration.[1] The event called to mind many aspects of the University's long history, including the prominence of Classical Studies in its curriculum. The University's catalogue for 1843 listed the following tuition and admissions requirements:

> For admission into the Freshman class, a candidate must have a correct knowledge of Cicero's orations, Virgil, John and the Acts in the Greek New Testament, Graeca Minora or Jacob's Greek Reader, English Grammar and Geography, and be well acquainted with Arithmetic . . . . Every candidate must be at least 14 years old . . . . The rate of Tuition, the Library Fee, and Servant's Hire, are $38 per annum, payable half yearly in advance.

Today the prospect of every college freshman knowing Latin and Greek seems nearly as incredible as an annual tuition of $38 (though the Louisiana State University Board of Supervisors, in setting a new two-year foreign language requirement for admission to the Baton Rouge campus beginning in 1988, urged the study of Latin in particular: Hargroder, reference no. 29, below). In the nineteenth century, however, such admissions policies were typical of colleges across the country. During the late 1800s, in fact, both the number and the percentage of high-school students enrolled in Latin rose dramatically: by the turn of the century more than 50% of our public secondary-school students were studying

[1] This paper has been adapted and substantially updated, by permission of the American Council on the Teaching of Foreign Languages (ACTFL), from my earlier and briefer *Foreign Language Annals* article, "1984: Latin in the United States Twenty Years After the Fall," reference no. 36, below; an intermediate revision also appeared in the 1984-85 Southern Conference on Language Teaching (SCOLT) proceedings, *Perspectives on Proficiency: Curriculum and Instruction* (ref. no. 37), and versions of the paper have been presented at meetings of SCOLT, the Classical Association of the Middle West and South—Southern Section, the Classical Associations of Florida and Virginia, the Alabama Classical Association, the Indiana Foreign Language Teachers Association, the National Junior Classical League, and the American Philological Association.

1

the language (about 263,000), and the actual number had increased to more than 899,000 by the mid-1930s.[2]

Fluctuations of interest and enrollments in Latin since that time, particularly over the past two decades, and some of the consequences of the ebb and flow, are the subject of the present study. Following a precipitous post-war decline to about 429,000 in 1948, secondary-school enrollments climbed steadily through 1962, when there were 702,000 public high-school students (grades 9-12) enrolled in Latin classes in this country (for these and other data cited in this paper, see the accompanying table, below, p. 15). Then, of course, came the Decade of the Relevant, the mid-1960s through the mid-1970s. Johnny did "his own thing" . . . and in the process forgot how to read and write; publishers revised college textbooks downward to a ninth-grade reading level; SAT scores dropped alarmingly. Public school Latin enrollments plummeted, falling 79%, from 702,000 in 1962 to a low of only 150,000 in 1976; while complete national enrollment figures are not available for private schools, their experience during this period seems to have been comparable, with an even more abrupt decline in parochial schools as a result of the de-emphasis of Latin by the Catholic Church. The number of Latin Achievement Test (AT) participants declined from 22,297 (1965) to 1,433 (1975), and Advanced Placement (AP) Exam participants fell from 1,208 in 1969 to about half that number in 1974. Membership in the National Junior Classical League (NJCL), the North American academic association for high-school Latin students sponsored by the American Classical League (ACL), fell from about 107,000 in 1964, to less than 29,000 a decade later. College enrollments in ancient Greek actually increased by more than 50% during the 1970s (partly, perhaps, as a result of the intense social consciousness of students of the period, to whom such characters as Socrates and Antigone were especially attractive), but college Latin dropped by over a third, from nearly 40,000 in 1965 to fewer than 25,000 in 1974. Membership in the ACL-sponsored National Senior Classical League (NSCL), an organization for college Latin students, also declined during this period, as did membership in most national and regional Classics professional associations (see table).[3]

To many it appeared that Latin, so long a cornerstone of the curriculum, especially the college-preparatory curriculum, was

[2] The source for all public high-school enrollment figures through 1978 cited in this study is Hammond and Scebold (28).

[3] AT and AP participation rates were obtained from the College Board; NJCL and NSCL figures, from the American Classical League. College enrollment data

destined to become indeed a "dead language." Foreign language study in general was, of course, one of a number of traditional academic areas weakened by educators and administrators of the period who demanded "relevancy" at every turn, challenged the concept of a core curriculum, and favored the cafeteria-line approach to high-school and college graduation requirements. Latin, that most ancient of relics, was naturally the first to go.

Over the last decade, however, the American public has become increasingly aware of the error in much of the educational reform of the 1960s and increasingly distressed at its consequences. The response of the 1970s was a cry that arose in near unison from parents, businessmen, educators, and even many students themselves for a movement "Back to Basics." Though that cry was at times perhaps too impassioned, though "the basics" were sometimes too narrowly defined, American education has unquestionably benefited from this movement and from the reassessment of curricular emphasis that followed. In 1979 the public's attention was drawn most sharply to the deplorable state of foreign language study in this country and to the crucial need for its revitalization in all of our schools, from the elementary through the university level, by the report of President Carter's Commission on Foreign Language and International Studies, *Strength through Wisdom* (Commission, ref. no. 9, below), and the imperative for foreign language study, as a means of enhancing general linguistic and communications skills as well as international cultural awareness, has been emphatically reasserted in the recommendations of subsequent national education study groups, including the Reagan/Bell Commission on Excellence in Education (National Commission, ref. 51) and the College Board's Educational Equality Project (Educational Equality, 17 and 18).

The classical languages, Latin in particular, have figured to one extent or another in virtually all of these discussions.[4] Moreover, during the late 1970s and the early 1980s considerable public interest was generated in Latin for its usefulness in improving English vocabulary and reading comprehension, as demonstrated in several research studies conducted during the period and widely reported in nationally circulated newspapers and magazines as well as in the professional journals.[5]

---

were provided by the Modern Language Association (MLA: and see below, n. 15); the MLA figures for Greek combine classical and biblical Greek (koine) and hence are not as meaningful as they might otherwise have been.

[4] See, for example, Educational EQuality Project (17, pp. 28-30); Lawall (40); LaBouve, et al. (32).

[5] See, for example, Masciantonio (45); Mavrogenes (46, 47); Sussman (66); Lehr

By 1976 interest in the study of Latin had reached its nadir in this country. In 1978 public high-school Latin enrollments rose, for the first time since 1962, to about 152,000. And by 1982, according to the most recent ACTFL survey available, they had increased again by nearly 13%, to approximately 170,000. This figure, it may be noted, represents an increase between 1978 and 1982 from 1.1% of total public secondary-school enrollments to 1.3%; by contrast, modern foreign language enrollments in grades 9-12 were down about 10%, from approximately 3 million to approximately 2.7 million and from 21.9% of total public secondary-school enroll-ments to 21.3%.[6]

There is good reason to suppose that the upward trend in Latin has continued since 1982, and that it could in fact continue for quite some time. Across the country there remains a strong interest in establishing new Latin programs and in revitalizing and ex-panding existing programs; in those states for which recent data are available, enrollments are still growing.[7] New and livelier methods and materials for teaching Latin are being developed, including the Cambridge Latin Course, Longman's *Ecce Romani* series, and a variety of computer-assisted instruction packages, to mention only a few.[8] NJCL memberships (which tend to parallel national enrollments), up by more than 25% from the 1977 low of 29,000 to about 37,000 in 1982, have in the last four years increased another 33%, to over 49,000 in 1986, the organization's 50th anniversary year;[9] participation in the College Board's Latin AT and AP exams continues to increase, and the number of partici-pants in the ACL's National Latin Exam has grown steadily from approximately 9,000 in 1978, when it was first instituted, to over 33,000 in 1982 and, by nearly 90% since then, to more than 60,000 in 1986.[10] News of this renaissance of interest and enrollments in

---

(41); Eddy (16); "Is Your English in Ruins?" (30); LaFleur (33, 35); Flaitz (19); "Latin Is Alive" (38); Bowen (4); Wiley (68).

[6] For the report on this ACTFL survey, see "Foreign Language Enrollments" (20); ACTFL is currently conducting a survey of fall, 1985, enrollments, the results of which are expected to appear in a fall, 1987, issue of *Foreign Language Annals*.

[7] In the state of New York, for example, public school Latin enrollments have risen dramatically over the past few years to more than 18,000 in 1984 (see Gascoyne, 22, p. 115); in Texas enrollments increased by 42% between 1981-82 and 1983-84 alone (see Wilhelm, below, p. 20) and a total of nearly 120% between 1976 and 1986 (Bogan, 3).

[8] See Phinney (57); Culley (10); Palma (55); LeMoine (42).

[9] The seven states with over 2,000 JCL members each are, with one exception, all southern states; the 1986 figures are TX 6,069, VA 5,908, FL 5,186, TN 3,529, GA 2,572, NC 2,239, and NJ 2,013.

[10] While the actual number of Latin students participating in the AT and AP

the language continues to appear unabated in both local and national media and provided a central focus for two summer, 1986, national conferences, the Wethersfield Institute conference, "Latin in Today's World," held September 5-7 at Columbia University, and an APA/ACL/NEH-sponsored conference on "The Classics in American Schools," held September 19-21 at the University of Virginia.[11]

Thus the Classics profession, educators in general, and the

---

exams has increased in recent years, the percentage of Latin students participating remains lamentably low, owing in large part, no doubt, to the fact that the vast majority of our students take only one or two years of the language and hence are unqualified, or feel unqualified, to sit for these exams: of the 95,625 Latin students (grades 9-12) reported for ACTFL's 1982 survey by states specifying level of language study, 84,645, or 88.5%, were enrolled in Latin I and II, with only 7,792 enrolled in Latin III courses, and fewer than 3,200 in Latin IV and above (see Wilhelm, Tab. 3, below, p. 22, rpt. from "Foreign Language Enrollments," 20, p. 620, Tab. 4D); less than 2,600 students took the Latin AT in 1982 and only about half that number sat for the Latin AP exam. Of the thousands of high-school Latin students in the 10 southeastern states comprising the College Board's Southern Region (KY, VA, TN, NC, SC, MS, AL, GA, LA, FL), a total of only 701 took the Latin AT during 1984-85: in Virginia, where about 15,000 students were enrolled in Latin, 393 took the exam; in Georgia, with an estimated 8,000 Latin students, only 38 sat for the exam (*College-Bound Seniors*, 8). For NLE participation rates, see National Latin Exam Committee (52). It should be mentioned too that, during the late 1960s and the 1970s, even before this period of increasing high-school Latin enrollments, a number of Latin FLES (Foreign Language in the Elementary Schools) programs were developed and became in some instances enormously successful, enrolling thousands of fourth-, fifth-, and sixth-graders, and attracting considerable public attention; see, for example, Masciantonio (45) and Mavrogenes (46, 47).

[11] As early as 1979 a *Newsweek* article (Sewall and Lee, 64, and cf. Greenfield, 26) heralded the "Return of the Classics" and predicted that "in the future, the crisis could be, *mirabile dictu*, a teacher shortage." Similar articles have appeared since then in numerous local and national periodicals including *U.S. News and World Report* ("Is Your English in Ruins? Take Latin!", 30), *Time* ("New Life for a Dead Language": Bowen, 4, and cf. "Pueri et Puellae Certantes," 60), the *Philadelphia Inquirer* (Pothier, 59), the *New York Times* ("Latin Is Alive," 38), the *Los Angeles Times* ("Renaissance in the Latin Language": Walsh, 67), and, most recently, *Newsweek on Campus* ("Classical Renaissance: Getting a Solid Education and Maybe Even a Job": Schwartz, 62), *Christian Science Monitor* ("Latin Redux, and Teachers Are Enthused," on the Wethersfield conference: Rowe, 61), and an Associated Press article published in newspapers around the country in the fall of 1986 (Gast, 23); see further the "Excerpta" and "In the News" columns regularly appearing for the past several years in, respectively, the *Classical Outlook* and the *ACL Newsletter*. Proceedings of the Wethersfield Institute conference will appear in a special issue of the journal *Helios* in 1987, edited by Professor Matthew Santirocco (Emory University), and the proceedings and recommendations of the University of Virginia conference have been edited by former ACL President Mary Ann Burns for publication by the Scholars Press, also in 1987.

public at large have succeeded in reviving in our schools what was, after all, never really a dead language. The greatest problem faced by the discipline in the 1980s, in fact, is that we have succeeded too well. As foreign language admissions requirements are being reinstituted at colleges and universities around the nation (e.g., in Arkansas, California, Colorado, Georgia, Louisiana, Massachusetts, Tennessee, and Texas), high schools are faced with the necessity— virtuous, but nonetheless difficult—of expanding existing language programs, or establishing new ones, and of finding the staff to direct them.[12] An increasingly critical shortage of qualified foreign language teachers, not unlike the current shortage of science and mathematics teachers, is rapidly developing in many states.[13]

In the case of Latin, with the number of students interested in the language steadily growing since the late 1970s, we have been faced with this shortage, in virtually every area of the country, for quite some time.[14] The growth in high-school Latin enrollments has unfortunately not been paralleled in our colleges. There are exceptions, of course: at the University of Georgia, Latin enrollments have tripled in the last few years, from about 250 to nearly 800, and some other institutions have enjoyed similar increases. Nationally, however, after a very modest 2.6% rise between 1977 and 1980, college Latin enrollments between 1980 and 1983 declined again by 3.2%, according to the latest MLA survey, released in the summer of 1984, to 24,224, the lowest number in this generation (see table).[15] Though we do not have certain

[12] On the rapidly accelerating trend toward more rigorous college admissions requirements, including foreign language requirements, during the 1980s, see especially Barthelmess (1); McCurdy (48); National Association of Secondary School Principals (50); Maeroff (43, 44); Scully (63); Gross (27); "New Requirements" (53); Draper (14, 15). According to the Carter Commission (Commission, 9, p. 6), the percentage of American colleges and universities with foreign language entrance requirements declined from 34% in 1966 to only 8% by the late 1970s; about 190, or 16%, of the nearly 1,200 colleges and universities responding to a 1981-82 survey conducted by the Illinois Foreign Language Teachers Association (IFLTA) indicated that they had such requirements (see Gerdisch, et al., 24), as did 178 (14.1%) of the 1,260 institutions surveyed by the MLA the following year (Brod and Lovitt, 5). Reports from and about numerous individual states and institutions during the period since the IFLTA and MLA surveys suggest that the figure has continued to rise: see, e.g., Draper (14, 15). Recent polls, it may be added, have indicated strong public support for foreign language requirements for college-bound students: see Gallup (21); Benderson (2, p. 6).

[13] See, e.g., "Catching Up with the Foreign Language Boom" (7); Digilio (13).

[14] See Lawall (39); Phinney (56, 58); Bowen (4); Wilhelm (70, rev. below, pp. 17-30); North (54); Digilio (13); Greenberg (25); and Schwartz (62).

[15] For a report on the 1980 survey, see Müller (49); for the 1983 survey, see Brod and Devens (6). Languages with the greatest gains between fall, 1980, and fall,

figures, all indicators (including a fall, 1984, survey of U.S. Classics departments conducted by ACL Placement Service Director Robert Wilhelm: see below, pp. 24-30) suggest that the number of Latin majors and minors, in decline during the late 1960s and the 1970s, has not increased significantly, if at all, during the first half of this decade, despite the growth of demand for secondary-school Latin teachers. Certainly the reports of the ACL's Placement Service and of the several local and regional Latin teacher placement services, as well as correspondence with foreign language coordinators from across the country, continue to indicate that position openings markedly, and distressingly, outnumber available candidates: in 1983-84, the ACL Placement Service advertised 186 openings in 30 states, but registered only 69 candidates; in 1984-85 there were 85 candidates for 236 positions; and in 1985-86 positions outnumbered candidates by 282 to 124.[16] In a survey of state foreign language coordinators which I conducted in fall, 1984, in connection with the preparation of a grant proposal to the National Endowment for the Humanities (to be discussed below), the 20 respondents unanimously affirmed the shortage of qualified Latin teachers in their states, in many instances terming the situation "severe," "critical," or "increasingly acute."

As a consequence of the lack of qualified teacher applicants, positions have often gone unfilled for a year, two years, or more, leaving an established program, and its students, in limbo; or enthusiastic plans for a new or expanded program have ultimately been abandoned. Or, as is happening all too frequently, persons unqualified, or at least seriously underqualified, have been hired or reassigned to make shift: the French teacher, or the English teacher, or the biology teacher, who, the ever-resourceful principal discovers, did study Latin—yes, indeed—for two years, in high

---

1983, were Japanese (+ 40.2%) and Russian (+ 26.7%); ancient Greek experienced the greatest decline (−12.5%). One can only assume that the MLA figures do have a relative reliability, from survey year to survey year; the figures shown for Latin and Greek in a given year, however, are probably lower than the actual count: as Brod and Devens indicate in their analysis of the 1983 report (6, p. 58), "It is likely that some [registrars and other college] officials omit data for ancient languages because they assume from the MLA's name that ancient languages are not to be included . . . . MLA cannot claim authoritative accuracy with respect to enrollments in these categories." An examination of the institutional data collected in the 1983 survey confirms that there were, indeed, a number of significant reporting omissions. Results of a survey of fall, 1986, enrollments will be available from MLA in 1987.

[16] See Wilhelm, below, pp. 17-30, and 69, summarized each year in the *Classical Outlook*; LaFleur (34, esp. p. 51).

school, 20 years ago, is appointed to the post and, presto, the school has a Latin program!

It is hard to judge which of these eventualities is the grimmest. For the student, a mediocre program may be worse than none at all. Certainly for the teacher, bright but inadequately prepared in the subject area, teaching "out of field" can be painfully frustrating, embarrassing, and demoralizing. Nevertheless, an increasing number of Latin classes in this country are being taught by persons lacking even minimal proficiency in the language and culture of ancient Rome, especially teachers who are reassigned by their principals to develop the new Latin courses necessitated by parent and student demand. In his 1981 report on the critical shortage of qualified Latin teachers, Professor Edward Phinney of the University of Massachusetts described his experiences teaching a course in Latin paedagogy at Tufts University's New England Classical Institute and Workshop (Phinney, 56, p. 1):

> ... nine of the twenty certified teachers enrolled had been recently reassigned by their school systems to teach Latin instead of English or a modern foreign language. Of these nine, none of whom was certified to teach Latin, five had not studied Latin in over a decade, two had studied it only a year or two, and two had not studied Latin at all (though they were scheduled to begin teaching Latin that September).

That the situation Professor Phinney describes is not unique to New England, and that it has not improved but worsened since he wrote his report in 1981, is confirmed by the experiences and testimony of teachers and school and college personnel from around the country. It may be noted that the NEH-funded Westminster Latin Institutes, an intensive program sponsored by Westminster College (New Wilmington, Pennsylvania) during the summers of 1984 and 1985 and designed to prepare underqualified Latin teachers for certification, attracted close to 300 inquiries and 78 completed applications for the 20 positions available (for a full report on the Westminster Institutes, see Dwight Castro, below, pp. 31-42).

In 1985 the National Endowment for the Humanities provided $249,860 for another National Institute, this one jointly sponsored by the American Classical League and the University of Georgia and designed in particular for this ever-growing group of "hybrid" Latin teachers—teachers who are bright, able, and motivated, but who lack the background in the language and culture of the Romans necessary for the development of a full Latin program. The Institute, described in detail below, pp. 43-62, consists of two intensive five-week sessions, held on the University of Georgia campus during the summers of 1986 and 1987, with a variety of continuation and follow-up activities scheduled for the 1986-87 and 1987-88 academic years while the participants are teaching in their home schools. Participants in the Institute receive intensive instruction in the language, from the beginning into the advanced level, and in aspects of the civilization, history, and literature of the Romans centering on the theme, "From Republic to Empire."

Applications for this Institute were accepted from current and prospective secondary-school teachers who had a firm, preferably contractual, commitment to teach Latin beginning in 1986 or 1987 but whose formal training in the language was insufficient to meet state certification requirements. Inquiries in response to the Institute announcement, which was distributed through a variety of media including notices for publication in about 70 professional journals and newsletters, totaled more than 500; over 400 application packets were distributed, 170 applications were initiated, and 125 completed applications were received. Only 25 participants could be selected, however, and this will surely not be enough to alleviate the shortage we are facing, a shortage which—in direct proportion to the success of our efforts at promoting interest in the language over the past decade—is becoming ever more critical.

While the situation we are facing today has the potential to create enormous difficulties, it has at the same time produced enormously promising opportunities. The job market for prospective high-school Latin teachers has been a seller's market for the past several years. And, as the nation's attention comes to focus ever more sharply on the crisis in American education, especially in secondary education, professional opportunities for Latin teachers should continue to improve. Society is becoming more and more appreciative of the need for academic excellence, and more and more willing to offer master teachers the respect, the improved working conditions, and the financial rewards they merit. We can now, in good conscience, earnestly exhort our students to consider Latin teaching as a profession.[17]

[17] While the focus of this study has been on the Latin teacher shortage at the secondary level, it should be noted that academic employment opportunities for Classics PhD's are also very good, relative to many other disciplines, and appear to be improving. According to the latest MLA survey of foreign language graduate programs (Devens and Bennett, 12), 75% of all 1983-84 recipients of the doctorate in Classics, i.e., 51 of 68 individuals, held full-time academic positions (half of them tenure-track positions) in 1984-85, a significantly higher percentage than the average for all language PhD's (60%: only Japanese, at 93%, and "Scandinavian," at 100% but with only two recipients, had higher full-time academic employment

The jobs are there, the conditions of the profession are improving; the students—Latin students—are motivated and disciplined above the average. It is among our foremost responsibilities today to recruit our high-school and college students to the study of the classical languages, to encourage the best of them to major or minor (with a second major, preferably, in another area), and to urge them to consider the many rewards of the teaching profession.

College and university classicists in particular need to be more aware of the serious problems in secondary Latin teaching today, and to be more concerned about those problems. We need to regard teacher preparation as a part of our professional responsibility just as important as publishing and teaching doctoral seminars. We need to appoint at least one faculty member in each college Classics department to serve as high-school liaison. We need to become familiar with our state's certification requirements and assist students with meeting those requirements and with the placement process. We need to collaborate with our colleagues in the modern languages and in the colleges of education. We need to offer courses whose content, scheduling, and location are appropriate to the needs of secondary-school teachers, including evening and weekend workshops, summer institutes, and classes on satellite campuses or in local school district facilities, designed with the current or prospective Latin teacher in mind. We need to be vigorous in pursuing support from state and national agencies such as the state Humanities Councils, the National Endowment for the Humanities, and the Fund for the Improvement of Post-secondary Education, as well as from private foundations and professional organizations interested in the improvement of secondary education.[18]

The imperative for these and other such efforts as are described in the following pages has not been greater, nor more urgent, nor more demonstrable, in this generation.[19]

---

rates). There are, moreover, indications that the job market will improve further during the early to mid-1990s, with the college-age population growing (see Wilhelm, below, p. 17) and a sizable number of current college faculty reaching retirement age (see Kitchell, below, p. 112; cf. Bagnall in Schwartz, 62).

[18] For a very helpful examination of "Recent Trends in Support by Private Foundations for Foreign Language Education," see Dandonoli (11); for information on support available from NEH and the state Humanities Councils, see the address provided at the end of this article (below, p. 11).

[19] Though considerations of space prohibit my doing so by name, I would like to thank again the many officers and staff members of ACTFL, MLA, ACL, APA, the College Board, and the several other national and regional organizations that have been so generous in providing the data analyzed in this study and compiled in the accompanying table.

For further information or assistance, write

President, American Classical League
Miami University
Oxford, OH 45056

Vice President for Educational Services
c/o American Philological Association
617 Hamilton Hall
Columbia University
New York, NY 10027

National Endowment for the Humanities
Overview of Programs—Room 409
1100 Pennsylvania Ave., NW
Washington, DC 20506

REFERENCES

1. Barthelmess, James A. "College and University Foreign Language Entrance Requirements." *Prospects* [newsletter of the ACL's National Committee for Latin and Greek, NCLG] 2 (1980): 1-4, and 3 (1980): 4-6.

2. Benderson, Albert. *Foreign Languages in the Schools.* Focus 12. Princeton, NJ: Educational Testing Service, 1983.

3. Bogan, Robert. "The Past Eight Decades of Latin in Texas Public Schools." *Texas Classics in Action* Summer 1986: 6-8.

4. Bowen, Ezra. "New Life for a Dead Language." *Time* 24 Dec. 1984: 61.

5. Brod, Richard I., and Carl R. Lovitt. "The MLA Survey of Foreign Language Entrance and Degree Requirements, 1982-83." *ADFL Bulletin* 15, iii (1984): 40-41.

6. Brod, Richard I., and Monica S. Devens. "Foreign Language Enrollments in U.S. Institutions of Higher Education—Fall 1983." *ADFL Bulletin* 16, ii (1985): 57-63.

7. "Catching Up with the Foreign Language Boom." *New York Times* 29 Dec. 1985: E9.

8. *College-Bound Seniors, 1985.* Southern, Georgia, and Virginia Reports. Atlanta, GA: CEEB Admissions Testing Program, 1985.

9. Commission on Foreign Language and International Studies. *Strength through Wisdom: A Critique of U.S. Capability.* Washington, DC: USGPO, 1979.

10. Culley, Gerald R. "The Delaware Latin Skills Project." *Classical Outlook* 62 (1984-85): 38-42.

11. Dandonoli, Patricia. "Recent Trends in Support by Private Foundations for Foreign Language Education." *Foreign Language Annals* 19 (1986): 49-56.

12. Devens, Monica S., and Nancy J. Bennett. "The MLA Surveys of

Foreign Language Graduate Programs, 1984-85." *ADFL Bulletin* 17, iii (1986): 19-27.

13. Digilio, Alice. "Language Classes Grow: New Requirements Bring Higher Enrollments, Teacher Shortages." *Washington Post* 11 Aug. 1985: "Education Review," 3.

14. Draper, J. B. "State Initiatives in Foreign Languages and International Studies." *Northeast Conference on the Teaching of Foreign Languages Newsletter* 16 (1984): 42-49.

15. ———, et al. "State Initiatives and Activities in Foreign Languages and International Studies." Washington, DC: Joint National Committee for Languages, Mar. 1986.

16. Eddy, Peter A. *The Effect of Foreign Language Study in High School on Verbal Ability as Measured by the Scholastic Aptitude Test—Verbal: Final Report.* Washington, DC: Center for Applied Linguistics, 1981.

17. Educational EQuality Project. *Academic Preparation for College: What Students Need to Know and Be Able to Do.* New York, NY: The College Board, 1983.

18. ———. *Academic Preparation in Foreign Language: Teaching for Transition from High School to College.* New York, NY: The College Board, 1986.

19. Flaitz, Jeffra. "Building the Basic Skills through Foreign Language in the Elementary School." *New York State Association of Foreign Language Teachers: Language Association Bulletin* 5, iii (1983): 1, 3-5.

20. "Foreign Language Enrollments in Public Secondary Schools, Fall 1982." *Foreign Language Annals* 17 (1984): 611-23.

21. Gallup, George H. "The 15th Annual Gallup Poll of the Public's Attitudes toward the Public Schools." *Phi Delta Kappan* 65 (1983): 41.

22. Gascoyne, Richard C. "Latin for Communication: The New York State Syllabus." *Classical Outlook* 63 (1986): 115-16.

23. Gast, Dorothy. "Resurgence of Latin Studies Causes Teacher Shortage." *Richmond Times-Dispatch* 5 Oct. 1986: D-19; this Associated Press article appeared in newspapers across the country, under a variety of titles, in fall, 1986.

24. Gerdisch, Marie-Rose, et al. *Foreign Languages in the Colleges and Universities of the United States.* Glenn Ellyn, IL: IFLTA, 1982.

25. Greenberg, Diane. "Rise in Latin Studies Outpaces Teachers." *New York Times* 27 Oct. 1985: Long Island sect.

26. Greenfield, Meg. "Back to the Ablative Absolute." *Newsweek* 12 Sept. 1977: 112.

27. Gross, Theodore. "Reviewing the Reports." *Change* 15, vii (1983): 34-43.

28. Hammond, Sandra B., and C. Edward Scebold. *Survey of Foreign Language Enrollments in Public Secondary Schools, Fall 1978.* New York, NY: ACTFL, 1980.

29. Hargroder, Charles M. "High School Requirements Are Toughened." *Times-Picayune/States-Item* [Baton Rouge, LA] 1 Feb. 1984: 1, 4.

30. "Is Your English in Ruins? Take Latin!" *U.S. News and World Report* 27 Apr. 1981: 58.

31. Jones, Lanie. "Study of Latin Language—Not Dead Yet." *Los Angeles Times* 12 Feb. 1980: pt. 1, pp. 1, 22.

32. LaBouve, Bobby, et al. "Classics and the Report of the President's Commission on Foreign Languages and International Studies." *Classical Outlook* 59 (1982): 104-13.

33. LaFleur, Richard A. "Latin Students Score High on SAT and Achievement Tests." *Classical Journal* 76 (1981): 254.

34. ———, et al. "Classics in the Middle West and South: An Update." *Classical Journal* 77 (1981): 49-64.

35. ———. "1981 SAT and Latin Achievement Test Results and Enrollment Data." *Classical Journal* 77 (1982): 343.

36. ———. "1984: Latin in the United States Twenty Years After the Fall." *Foreign Language Annals* 18 (1985): 341-47; shorter, preliminary version of the present study.

37. ———. "The Study of Latin in American Schools: Success and Crisis." In *Perspectives on Proficiency: Curriculum and Instruction.* Ed. T. B. Fryer and F. W. Medley. Columbia, SC: SCOLT, 1986; shorter, preliminary version of the present study. 73-82.

38. "Latin Is Alive and Well in Grade School." *New York Times* 9 Jan. 1983: "Winter Survey of Education" sect., pp. 25-26.

39. Lawall, Gilbert. "Teacher Training and Teacher Placement: Responsibilities of the Colleges and Universities to the Schools." *Classical World* 72 (1979): 409-15.

40. ———. "The President's Commission and Classics: Recommendations and Strategies for Their Implementation." *Classical Outlook* 57 (1980): 73-79.

41. Lehr, Fran. "Latin Study: A Promising Practice in English Vocabulary Instruction?" *Journal of Reading* 22 (1979): 76-79; rpt. in *Classical Outlook* 57 (1980): 87-88.

42. LeMoine, Fannie J. "Classics, the Academy, and the Community." *Federation Reports* [Journal of the State Humanities Councils] May 1984, Special Issue: 22–27; rpt. in *Classical Outlook* 63 (1985): 6-9.

43. Maeroff, Gene I. "Ties That Do Not Bind." *Change* 14, i (1982): 12-17.

44. ———. *School and College: Partnerships in Education.* Princeton, NJ: Carnegie Foundation for the Advancement of Teaching, 1983.

45. Masciantonio, Rudolph. "Tangible Benefits of the Study of Latin." *Foreign Language Annals* 10 (1977): 375-82.

46. Mavrogenes, Nancy A. "The Effect of Latin on Language Arts Performance." *Elementary School Journal* 77 (1977): 268-73.

47. ———. "Latin in the Elementary School: A Help for Reading and Language Arts." *Phi Delta Kappan* 60 (1979): 675-77; rpt. in *Classical Outlook* 57 (1979): 33-35.

48. McCurdy, Jack. "Sending the Message: New Admissions Standards for a New Decade." *Phi Delta Kappan* 63 (1982): 547-50.

49. Müller, Kurt E. "Foreign Language Enrollments in U.S. Institutions of Higher Education—Fall, 1980." *ADFL Bulletin* 13, ii (1981): 31-34.

50. National Association of Secondary School Principals. *College Admissions: New Requirements by the State Universities.* Reston, VA: NASSP, 1982.

51. National Commission on Excellence in Education. *A Nation at Risk.* Washington, DC: USGPO, 1983.

52. National Latin Exam Committee. "The National Latin Exam: 1978-85." *Classical Outlook* 62 (1984-85): 45-47.

53. "New Requirements for High School Graduates." *ACTFL Public Awareness Network Newsletter* 3, i (1984): 2-3.

54. North, Helen F. "Report of the American Philological Association." In *A Report to the Congress of the United States of America on the State of the Humanities.* New York, NY: American Council of Learned Societies, 1985. 74-81.

55. Palma, Ronald B. "*Ecce Romani*: A Preview of the North American Revision." *Classical Outlook* 62 (1984-85): 42-44.

56. Phinney, Edward. "The Critical Shortage of Qualified Latin Teachers." *Prospects* 4 (1981): 1-2; rpt. in *Classical Outlook* 59 (1981): 10-11.

57. ———. "Revision of the Cambridge Latin Course: An Update." *Classical Outlook* 59 (1981): 6-7.

58. ———. "Building Professional Development Programs for Classics Teachers." *Classical Outlook* 59 (1982): 110-13.

59. Pothier, Dick. "Latin, a 'Dead Language,' Roars Back to Life." *Philadelphia Inquirer* 13 Nov. 1982: 1-2B.

60. "Pueri et Puellae Certantes." *Time* 15 Aug. 1977: 82.

61. Rowe, Jonathan. "Latin Redux, and Teachers Are Enthused." *Christian Science Monitor* 15 Sept. 1986: 16-17.

62. Schwartz, John. "Classical Renaissance: Getting a Solid Education and Maybe Even a Job." *Newsweek on Campus* Mar. 1986: 52.

63. Scully, Malcolm G. "Raising College Standards Is Already in the Works." *Chronicle of Higher Education* 11 May 1983: 1, 10.

64. Sewall, Gil, and Elliott D. Lee. "Return of the Classics." *Newsweek* 12 Nov. 1979: 126.

65. Study Group on the Conditions of Excellence in American Higher Education. *Involvement in Learning: Realizing the Potential of American Higher Education.* Washington, DC: USGPO, 1984.

66. Sussman, Lewis A. "The Decline of Basic Skills: A Suggestion So Old That It's New." *Classical Journal* 73 (1978): 346-52.

67. Walsh, Elsa. "Renaissance in the Latin Language." *Los Angeles Times* 23 Nov. 1984: V-A, 10.

68. Wiley, Patricia D. "High School Foreign Language Study and College Academic Performance." *Classical Outlook* 62 (1984-85): 33-36.

69. Wilhelm, Robert M. "Annual Report of the Director of the ACL Placement Service for Latin and Greek." In *American Classical League Annual Reports of Officers and Committee Chairmen.* Oxford, OH: ACL, 1984-86.

70. ———. "The Shortage of Latin Teachers: Fact or Fiction?" *Classical Outlook* 62 (1985): 105-10; rev. below, pp. 17-30.

LATIN ENROLLMENTS, CLASSICAL ASSOCIATION MEMBERSHIPS, AND LATIN/GREEK EXAM PARTICIPANTS
1960–1986

	Enrollments			Memberships											Participants			
	H.S. Latin[1]	College Latin[2]	College Greek[2] (Ancient)	NJCL[1]	NSCL	ACL	APA	CAMWS Area[3]	CAMWS Total[4]	CAAS[5]	CAPN	CANE	AIA	CAC	National Latin Exam	Latin AT	Latin AP	National Greek Exam
1960	654,670	25,700[6]	12,700[6]	107,086				2192	4363			892	2746			10,048	208	
1961	695,297			101,810				2296	4577			930	3014			13,474	352	
1962	702,135						1568	2378	4696			933	3404			16,980	439	
1963	680,234						1685	2541	5027			929	3693			17,788	677	
1964	590,047					6252	1784	2591	5143			921	3868			20,244	862	
1965	591,445	39,600[7]	19,500[7]		213	6120	1855	2649	5184			934	4202			22,297	885	
1966				98,201	448	6064	2053	2736	5239			954	4520			20,670	984	
1967				88,727	694	5855	2175	2698	5112			973	5173			19,561	882	
1968	371,977	34,981	17,516			5812	2355	2768	5244			906	5996	560		18,462	971	
1969					766	5209	2468	2682	5205			904	6446	518		15,920	1208	
1970	265,293	27,591	16,697			4465	2586	2606	4816			841	6753	582		12,777	1046	
1971				39,772		4118	2770	2600	4618			780	6867	580		7,460	975	
1972				36,890		3872	2765	2512	4449			730	6889	619		5,425	853	
1973				32,918	674	3444	2837	2231	3968		124	752	6695	636		4,231	705	
1974	167,165	25,167	24,391	28,894	610	3562	2861	1991	3524		127	724	6202	667		3,049	611	
1975				30,532		3469	2900	1916	3443		129	714	5752	547		1,433	624	
1976	150,470			28,870	632	2970	2928	1872	3535		125	651	6063	562		1,555	745	
1977		24,403	25,843	29,010	543	2814		1834	3357		132	641	6999	554		1,734	841	
1978	151,782			31,152		2771	2864	1754	3100		122	576	7601	548	9,000[8]	1,725	880	
1979				32,026		2890	2855	1654	3071		125	616	7923	542	16,497	1,649	1016	
1980		25,035	22,111	33,924	600	2880	2847	1618	2915		141	606	8758	559	20,710	2,060	1122	
1981				37,017		3006	2932	1657	2881		120	645	9680	557	27,602	2,258	1261	310
1982	169,580			40,574	659	2995	3025	1575	2753		109	662	8981	559	33,336	2,587	1311	415
1983		24,224	19,350	44,452	643	2980	3025	1611	2757	643	107	712	8717	548	35,604	2,455	1529	597
1984				48,350	550	3061	3087	1651	2805	630	99	756	8645	530	46,565	2,685	1704	545
1985				49,489	525[8]	3088		1613	2682	682	120	777	8739	535	53,505	2,865	1929	639
1986					478	3472	2890	1637	2809	675	106	810	8668		60,026	3,140	2104	752

Abbreviations: NJCL, National Junior Classical League; NSCL, National Senior Classical League; ACL, American Classical League; APA, American Philological Association; CAMWS, Classical Association of the Middle West and South; CAAS, Classical Association of the Atlantic States; CAPN, Classical Association of the Pacific Northwest; CANE, Classical Association of New England; AIA, Archaeological Institute of America; CAC, Classical Association of Canada; Latin AT, the College Board's Latin Achievement Test; Latin AP, the College Board's Latin Advanced Placement Exam.

[1] Source: ACTFL. [2] Source: MLA. [3] Includes only members in the thirty CAMWS states and two Canadian provinces. [4] Includes, in addition to CAMWS area members, subscribers to the Classical Journal (the association's journal) from outside CAMWS territory. [5] Figures before 1983 currently unavailable from CAAS headquarters. [6] Estimated by MLA. [7] Rounded to the nearest hundred by MLA. [8] Approximate.

The Shortage of High-School Latin Teachers

Robert McKay Wilhelm
Miami University

Between 1939 and 1981 approximately 6.1 million individuals aged 21 to 65 had completed teacher certification requirements in the United States, according to statistics published by the National Education Association (NEA: *Teacher Supply and Demand*, 17, p. 19). According to that same report (p. 23, Tab. 5), the number of new college graduates with teacher certification declined steadily from an all-time high of 317,254 in 1972 to a low of 140,639 in 1981, resulting in a 44% decrease in the supply of teachers in all fields at the elementary and secondary levels. The demand for teachers is generally measured in two ways: 1) *actual demand*, the number of teachers required in any given year to fill available positions; 2) *quality demand*, the number of teachers required in any given year in order to raise the quality of the school programs to minimum levels. In fall, 1981, the actual demand for new teachers was 109,550, but it was estimated by the NEA that 426,850 new teachers would be required "if school programs and services were raised to minimum quality levels immediately" (*Teacher Supply and Demand*, 17, p. 12).

In the 1985 edition of *The Condition of Education* (U.S. Department of Education, 18, p. 3) student enrollment was projected to increase steadily in the late 1980s and early 1990s. Student enrollment at the elementary level (K-8) was projected to decrease to 30.9 million in 1985; reversing the decline of the 1970s and the early 1980s, an upward trend was expected to begin in 1986 and to reach a peak of 35.4 million by 1993, an increase of 14% above the 1985 figure. Enrollment in grades 9-12 is expected to decrease during this same period, reaching 12.3 million by 1992, 12% below the 1982 figure. By 1993, however, the students from the lower grades will have reached the upper level and the 1986-93 increase experienced at the elementary level will begin to appear in grades 9-12. Between 1988 and 1992 the demand for additional and new teachers is expected to increase to 924,000, when the children of the "baby boomers" reach middle-school and high-school level. A recent Carnegie Task Force has made similar projections, estimating that 1.3 million new teachers will be needed over the next decade; to meet the need, 23% of college graduates would have to enter the teaching profession during that period, nearly four times the 6.2% of rising college freshmen who indicated in a recent survey their interest in teaching careers (Carnegie, 4, pp. 26, 31, and see further "Databank," 5; Empey, 6; Ferris and Winkler, 7; Masland and Williams, 11; Olson and Rodman, 14; and Rush, 16).

What about the supply and demand for Latin teachers? From 1961 to 1973 the NEA, for its yearly *Teacher Supply and Demand* surveys, collected data on the number of students graduating with Latin certification (see Tab. 1, col. 2, below). According to these data, provided to the author by NEA's Teacher Supply and Demand Project Director, William S. Graybeal, there were 270 graduates with certification in Latin in 1961. In 1964, when NEA surveyed 573 four-year colleges and universities and 53 junior colleges, there were 390 graduates certified to teach Latin, and the number rose to 464 in 1965.

During the early 1960s, job opportunities for graduating students were plentiful, it is generally agreed; but statistics regarding placement of graduates are elusive and hopelessly incomplete at best. In 1966-67 the American Classical League (ACL), under the direction of Executive Secretary John F. Latimer, received a grant from the National Endowment for the Humanities (NEH) in order to analyze the current situation of Latin instruction in the secondary schools, to estimate teacher supply and demand, and to publish a report offering guidelines and recommendations for action. In *The Oxford Conference and Related Activities: A Report to The National Endowment for the Humanities*, Latimer reported that in 1966-67 placement offices in 54 colleges and universities received nearly 3,000 requests for foreign language teachers; it was impossible, Latimer noted, to determine how many were Latin positions (Latimer, 10, pp. 93-94). The number of positions must have been substantial, however, considering the fact that there were approximately 500,000 public high-school students enrolled in Latin, 98,201 members of the National Junior Classical League, 5,855 ACL members, 19,561 students who took the Latin Achievement Test, and 882 who took the Latin Advanced Placement Exam (see table in LaFleur, 9, above, p. 15).

NEA's yearly *Teacher Supply and Demand* surveys revealed a precipitous decrease in the number of graduates certified in Latin between 1969, when there were 452, and 1973, when the number had declined to only 133. The number of newly certified teachers in all foreign languages also declined during the period, but the greatest losses were in Latin (Tab. 1, col. 1-2), since the language

TABLE 1: Teaching Certificates, Degrees, and ACL-Listed Teaching Positions in Latin/Classics

Year	Certified in Foreign Language [1]	Certified in Latin [2]	BA Latin [3]	MA Latin [3]	PhD Latin. [3]	BA Classics [3]	MA Classics [3]	PhD Classics [3]	ACL-Listed Teaching Positions [4]
1960	2,178								
1961		270							
1962	3,227	332	886	183					
1963		351							
1964	5,281	390	1,058 (est)	288 (est)					
1965		464	1,114	310					
1966	7,162	390	1,245	361					
1967		390 (est)							
1968	9,015	438							
1969		452							
1970	9,640	320							
1971	9,928	270	463	132	5	341	110	57	
1972	9,323	160	337	77	8	403	123	58	
1973	8,932	133	274	46	7	354	117	58	
1974	8,452	147 (est)	311	63	6	450	126	46	
1975	7,046	30 (Tx)[5]	208	52	2	481	118	74	
1976	6,093	25 (Tx)	169	42	2	483	136	61	
1977	5,763	20 (Tx)	120	22	3	491	133	41	
1978	5,060	22 (Tx)	117	14	2	441	132	57	115
1979	4,500	25(Tx) + [20][6] = 45	110	24	1	411	103	47	
1980	2,550	7 (Tx) + [17] = 24	95	14	2	404	97	44	114
1981	2,190	14 (Tx) + [19] = 33	98	20	4	403	88	50	86
1982		19 (Tx) + [20] = 39	86	10	2	381	133	48	47
1983		11 (Tx) + [22] = 33	[80]			[199]			106
1984		26 (Tx) + [26] = 52	[89]			[172]			186
1985		[39]							
1986		[31]							236
1987		[13]							
1988		[7]							282

[1] Statistics obtained from *Teacher Supply and Demand in Public Schools*, 1962–82.
[2] Statistics supplied by William S. Graybeal, NEA Project Director of *Teacher Supply and Demand in Public Schools*.
[3] Data from *Digest of Education Statistics*, 1960–85, National Center for Education Statistics.
[4] Statistics from Annual Reports of R.M. Wilhelm, Director of ACL Placement Service, 1978–86 (ref. 19).
[5] Statistics for Texas supplied by Bobby LaBouve, Director, Second Language Division, Texas Education Agency.
[6] Numbers marked [ ] are derived from the fall, 1984. ACL Certification Survey.

was being increasingly regarded as "irrelevant" and "dead" and therefore useless in the modern world. The drop in the number of newly certified Latin teachers followed closely the decline in high-school Latin enrollments from a high of 702,135 in 1962 to 167,165 in 1974 and a low of 150,470 in 1976 (Tab. 2); the plight of the profession at large is reflected in the reduced membership of almost every classical organization during this period (see LaFleur, 9, above, p. 15).

Since 1978, however, the downward trend in Latin enrollments has slowly begun to reverse itself. Figures released in December, 1984, by the American Council on the Teaching of Foreign Languages (ACTFL) revealed that by 1982 public high-school enrollments in Latin had risen to 169,580, reflecting a 12.7% increase over the 1976 figure ("Foreign Language Enrollments," 8). The ACTFL language study relied on reported fall, 1982, data for grades 7-12 from 32 states and the District of Columbia; some states submitted fall, 1981, data, and others reported only grades 9-12 or only the totals for the various languages, not broken down by grade level (see Tab. 2 and 3). Enrollments were estimated for the 18 missing states. It should be noted that the ACTFL statistics do not include the enrollments from private and church-related schools and hence give only an incomplete picture of the total number of students studying Latin in the United States; moreover, figures provided to the author by several state foreign language consultants indicate enrollments for fall, 1982, higher than those reported by ACTFL (e.g., in Texas the numbers were considerably higher; in Virginia enrollments totaled 13,560 instead of 13,010).

There is every reason to believe that this upward movement has continued since 1982; for example, in Virginia the 1983-84 enrollment rose to 15,311, a 13% increase over the 1982 figure; in Florida the 1983-84 enrollment was 7,234, a 15% increase; in Texas the 1983-84 enrollment was 12,438, a 42% increase over 1981-82, and the 1985-86 enrollment reached 16,027, a 123% increase over the 1979-80 figure of 7,212. The dramatic growth in the number of students joining the National Junior Classical League (from 37,017 to 49,489 between 1980 and 1986) and of those taking the National Latin Examination (from 33,336 to 60,026 over the same period) is also a good barometer of increasing high-school enrollments (see LaFleur, 9, above).

In January, 1985, the Modern Language Association (MLA) reported that 24,224 students were enrolled in Latin at the college level in the fall of 1983 (Brod and Devens, 3). This figure, based on replies from 518 four-year colleges and 30 two-year colleges and including 22,893 undergraduates and 894 graduates enrolled in

TABLE 2: Latin Enrollment in the United States and Ontario, Canada

| Year | H.S. Latin Enrollment Ontario[1] | H.S. Latin Enrollment United States[2] | College Latin Enrollment in the United States[3] | | | |
			Two-Year Undergrad.	Four-Year Undergrad.	Graduate	Total
1960		654,670				25,700
1961		695,297				
1962		702,135				
1963		680,234				
1964		590,047				39,600
1965		591,445				
1966						
1967						
1968		371,977	1,450	32,072	1,459	34,981
1969						
1970		265,293	667	25,559	1,365	27,591
1971						
1972			357	22,837	1,204	24,398
1973						
1974		167,165	460	23,544	1,163	25,167
1975	19,668					
1976	18,941	150,470				
1977	15,745		429	22,965	1,009	24,403
1978	14,307	151,782				
1979	14,746					
1980	13,325		566	23,684	785	25,035
1981	12,573					
1982	9,859	169,580				
1983	10,371		437	22,893	894	24,224
1984	10,287					

[1] Source: Ontario Classical Association.
[2] From "Foreign Language Enrollments," 8, p. 613.
[3] Detailed statistics supplied by Richard I. Brod, Director, MLA Foreign Language Programs.

21

TABLE 3: Latin Enrollments by State and Level of Instruction, Grades 7–12 and 9–12*

LATIN	Level I		Level II	Level III	Level IV	Level V	Level VI	Unspecified		Total Reported	
	Grades 7 & 8	Grades 9-12	Level II	Level III	Level IV	Level V	Level VI	Grades 9-12	Grades 7-12	Grades 9-12	Grades 7-12
STATES REPORTING	8,389	55,078	29,567	7,792	2,780	400	8	12,496	1,949	108,121	118,459
Alaska	33	42	25							67	100
Arizona	0	190	121	14	3					328	328
Arkansas	127	250	177	18					69	445	641
California	0	2,554	2,554	385	384					5,877	5,877
Colorado	20	778	538	92	27	13				1,448	1,468
Connecticut	259	3,687	1,739	632	216	24	8			6,306	6,565
Delaware	10	115	40	19	7					181	191
District of Columbia	241	531	52	5	4					592	833
Florida	0	4,296	1,657	273	79	21				6,326	6,326
Hawaii	0	20	32	5						57	57
Illinois	245	2,546	1,840	434	212	18				5,050	5,295
Indiana	0	3,280	1,683	582	123	36				5,704	5,704
Iowa	0	206	110	12	3					331	331

State										
Kansas	0	742	173	31	6	3			955	955
Kentucky	0	1,696	656	22	30				2,404	2,404
Louisiana	0							681		681
Minnesota	28	382	104	41	21				548	576
Missouri	0	1,021	439	237					1,697	1,697
Montana	0	127	126	48	47				348	348
Nebraska	0							941		941
New Hampshire	17	1,508	578	245	62	34			2,427	2,444
New York	2,799	6,603	3,325	1,696	378	175	1,360		13,537	16,336
North Carolina	0	3,200	1,600	300	100				5,200	5,200
North Dakota	0	191	66	17					274	274
Ohio	0						11,136		11,136	11,136
Pennsylvania	1,981	6,159	3,672	793	390				11,014	12,995
South Carolina	0	1,650	654	46					2,350	2,350
Texas	205	5,339	2,047	447	78				7,911	8,116
Utah	0							258		258
Vermont	82	845	415	110	34	1			1,405	1,487
Virginia	2,024	5,191	4,207	1,087	426	75			10,986	13,010
West Virginia	97	855	377	13	2				1,247	1,344
Wisconsin	221	1,074	560	188	148				1,970	2,191

*From "Foreign Language Enrollments," 8, p. 620; reprinted by permission of ACTFL.

four-year institutions and 437 students enrolled in two-year colleges, is 3.2% lower than that reported in MLA's 1980 survey (25,035: see Tab. 2). The 1983 figure should be higher, however: an examination of the detailed statistics collected by MLA has revealed that the survey was frozen before a number of institutions had reported their enrollments and that in some instances enrollments were reported incorrectly.

Over the past few years the American Classical League has been increasingly concerned with Latin enrollment trends and with Latin teacher supply and demand. Edward Phinney, in his article "The Critical Shortage of Qualified Latin Teachers," noted that "whatever the reason for the shortage of qualified Latin teachers, the shortage does exist. It is important now that the many Latin-teacher training programs in the United States be reactivated and that the recruitment of future Latin teachers be given high priority" (Phinney, 15, p. 2). As Director of the ACL's Latin/Greek Teacher Placement Service, I was asked by Professor Richard LaFleur, President of the ACL (1984-86), to conduct during the fall of 1984 a survey of all college and university Classics and foreign language departments in the United States and Canada in order to obtain statistics regarding the number of graduates in Latin during the past five years and the number projected to graduate in Latin during the next four years, as well as the perceived demand for Latin teachers in the respondents' states.

In September, 1984, a questionnaire and cover letter were mailed first class (with self-addressed, stamped return envelope) to 435 Classics and foreign language departments in the United States and to 56 departments in Canada. Among the specific questions asked were the following: 1) number of students graduated with a BA in Latin 1979-84; 2) number of students graduated with a BA in Classics 1979-84; 3) number of students currently majoring in Latin, freshmen through seniors; 4) number of students currently majoring in Classics, freshmen through seniors; 5) number of students graduated with teacher certification in Latin 1979-84; 6) number of students graduated with teacher certification in a double major; 7) number of students currently seeking teacher certification in Latin, freshmen through seniors; 8) What does your department do to recruit and encourage students to consider a career in Latin language teaching at the secondary- or elementary-school level? 9) Has your department been contacted by a superintendent of schools or a school principal regarding the hiring of a Latin teacher? If yes, what did the department do to help? 10) From your perspective, what is your best estimate concerning the number of teachers available to teach Latin at the elementary- or secondary-school level?

The response rate from the Canadian universities was only 16% with the greatest number of replies coming from the province of Ontario. High-school Latin in Ontario experienced a 50% drop in enrollment between 1974 and 1981, from 19,668 to 9,859; since then there has been a modest increase in the Latin enrollments, with an additional 928 students in the province enrolled in Classical Civilization courses. There are approximately 200 schools in Ontario which offer a Latin program either in French or in English. Since Ontario launched its so-called "Back-to-Basics" high-school curriculum in fall, 1984—with almost twice as many compulsory subjects as before and the right to graduate after four years instead of five—many teachers of third languages are fearful that they may be left behind as students rush through school concentrating on 16 compulsory subjects out of the 30 credits which are required to graduate. During the summer of 1984 the Ontario Ministry of Education co-sponsored with the Ontario Classical Association a Classics Seminar to design new Ontario academic courses in Greek, Latin, and Classical Civilization to replace existing Grade 13 courses. As the new blueprint for education in the Ontario schools is unfolded, Paul Whalen, Vice President of the Ontario Classical Association, reports that "Latin teachers in Ontario are alive, well, enthusiastic, but vigilant." The alarming aspect of the Ontario situation is that for many years there were no active Latin teacher certification programs at any of the colleges of education. "For these reasons," as Ross Kilpatrick, Chair of the Department of Classics at Queen's University in Kingston, commented in 1984, "our students do not *think* of teaching." The Faculty of Education at Queen's University, however, has now introduced a course for 1987-88 leading to professional qualifications in Latin for Ontario teachers.

The reply rate to the ACL survey from American universities was 44%, a good response that likely included most departments at all active in training prospective Latin teachers. Of the 191 departments replying, 33 departments (18%) reported that Latin was not offered; 31 (16%) stated that it was impossible to be certified in Latin at their universities; another 68 reported that they had not certified a single student in Latin in the last five years; and several reported that not within living memory had they ever had a student earn certification in Latin. Only 59 institutions reported graduating students with certification in Latin between 1979 and 1984: the number of those graduates appears to be depressingly low and the number expected to graduate over the next four years is likewise a cause for concern (Tab. 1). The very serious issues regarding Latin teacher preparation raised by Phinney in 1981 are still confronting us today, and "the classical education of America's young people hangs in the balance" (Phinney, 15, p. 2).

It appears from the ACL survey that there are certain states and universities throughout the country where teacher certification in Latin is of considerable importance. For example, between 1979 and 1984 the University of Massachusetts graduated 26 MAT students in Latin and Classical Humanities. At the University of Michigan 22 students were graduated with certification during that same period, and 5 others were expected to graduate in 1985; 15 were graduated with certification from the College of William and Mary; 9 from Radford University; and 8 from the University of Georgia.

By far the most prolific producer of certified Latin teachers has been the state of Texas, where there are 12 approved teacher education programs in Latin at the following colleges and universities: Austin College, Baylor University, North Texas State University, Southwestern University, Texas Tech University, the University of Houston at University Park, the University of Texas at Austin, the University of Texas at Dallas, the University of Dallas, the University of St. Thomas, William Marsh Rice University, and Trinity University. Representatives from these institutions, as well as the Director of Languages for the Texas Education Agency, Mr. Bobby LaBouve, meet each November at the Annual Texas Conference on the Recruitment, Training, and Placement of Latin Teachers. Precise statistics are available for teachers gaining Latin certification in Texas since 1972-73 (see Tab. 1). Furthermore, the Texas Latin Teacher Placement Service, under the direction of Professor Karl Galinsky from the University of Texas at Austin, very carefully monitors the demand for teachers. During 1983-84, 30 Texas schools notified the Service of vacancies; 23 candidates with various restrictions regarding mobility were listed with the Placement Service. Only 15 of the 30 vacancies were filled, and some of the schools pressed into service teachers with minimal qualifications in the language. There are approximately 200 Latin teachers and 100 districts offering Latin in Texas, and enrollments are continuing to rise. Mr. LaBouve estimates "that Texas will need at least 30 new Latin teachers each year for the next five to ten years. The projected shortfall is horrendous and will quickly stunt our growth in enrollment unless there is a miracle."

It is such increases in language enrollments that have caused educators and administrators to worry about the shortage of teachers. In a recent article published in *Education Week* (Bridgman, 2), Alfred Gage, Specialist for Foreign Language Education in the Oklahoma State Department of Education, is quoted as saying, "I'm getting calls every day from school administrators who want to hire foreign language teachers, and we don't have them. We're in a bind . . . [and] we'll be in a bind for a while. We've only been graduating 12 to 15 foreign-language teachers [a year] from teacher-training institutions." In his reply to the fall, 1984, ACL survey, Mr. Gage wrote, "We've had very few young people in teacher education programs in Latin and, consequently, as our older teachers retire we've had to see a number of programs eliminated. In almost every case, it was *not* the choice of the school administration. I have received desperate calls from school principals who are seeking a Latin teacher, but I've usually not been able to help them. . . . Unfortunately the Classics Department of the University of Oklahoma is the only institution in Oklahoma which has a teacher education program in Latin."

The Oklahoma situation is matched by that of a number of other states throughout the nation. In Virginia, Helen P. Warriner-Burke, Associate Director for Foreign Languages, ESL, and Bilingual Education, reported that "Latin teachers are as scarce as the proverbial hen's teeth." High-school Latin enrollments in Virginia are increasing rapidly and Warriner-Burke estimated that the state will need "approximately 50 new Latin teachers during the next five years and equally that many more during the subsequent five years." Florida has also experienced a teacher shortage in Latin as a result of a 38% increase in enrollments: to alleviate the shortage, the state has funded summer institutes to provide opportunities for persons teaching out of field to become certified, as well as to improve the language skills of teachers already certified. Gabriel M. Valdes, Foreign Language Program Specialist in Florida's Department of Education, described these programs: "State grants are provided to students preparing to become foreign language teachers and who pledge to teach in Florida schools for three years after graduation. New teachers are entitled to payment by the state of any school loan they received during their preservice years. Practicing teachers can take courses to become certified in an area of teacher shortage and the state will reimburse their tuition. Persons holding a bachelor's degree in an area of teacher shortage can become certified after a year in a beginning teacher program without taking education courses." In Connecticut there are over 100 Latin teachers in the public schools, where Latin enrollments are steadily increasing. Six districts in the state reported to the Foreign Language and ESOL Consultant, Kenneth A. Lester, that they had difficulty finding candidates for Latin vacancies. In a letter to the Director of the ACL Placement Service, Mr. Lester expressed a grave concern: "The disturbing point is that we have prepared no Latin teachers in the state's teacher preparation institutions in the last two or three years." The Foreign Language Consultant from Georgia, Greg Duncan, stated that "in every corner of the state Latin enrollments are increasing tremendously and systems are experiencing difficulty in locating qualified teachers. Part-time Latin teachers have now been scheduled to full-day Latin duties; teachers who have not taught Latin in years are being called back for assistance"; of 15 openings for 1984-85 listed with the Georgia Classical Association's Placement Service, several were not filled. In New York the implementation of the proposed Regents Action Plan will mean that many more students in the state will be studying foreign languages, including Latin and Greek. Richard C. Gascoyne, Associate for Latin and Greek in the Bureau of Foreign Languages Education, New York State Education Department, stated that in New York "there is already a shortage of Latin teachers; there is every indication that this shortage will become more acute with the implementation of the Regents Action Plan." Indeed, during 1985-86 the state of New York advertised more than 80 Latin teaching positions with the ACL Placement Service. In letters from foreign language consultants in West Virginia, Washington, Alabama, Illinois, Kentucky, Ohio, Montana, New Hampshire, and Vermont, four points about the teacher shortage problem were repeated consistently: 1) more high-school students are studying foreign languages as part of the Back to Basics movement; 2) high-school Latin enrollments are increasing; 3) there is a shortage of Latin teachers; 4) not enough students are graduating with Latin certification to meet the demand.

The shortage of teachers described by the foreign language consultants is reflected in the requests for teachers sent to the ACL's Latin/Greek Teacher Placement Service, the only national placement office which maintains an applicant file of individuals seeking Latin teaching positions at the secondary and elementary levels. During the month of August, 1984, the Placement Service received calls almost daily from superintendents and principals all over the country; one principal even made a 250-mile trip to the office in order to go through all applicant files, so committed was he to seeing that Latin would continue to be offered in his school. The ACL Placement Service advertised a total of 186 jobs during 1983-84, but registered only 69 persons seeking positions; in 1984-85 there were 85 candidates for 236 positions, and in 1985-86 124 candidates for 282 positions. The number of positions listed by the New England Latin Placement Service has also exceeded the number of registered candidates over the past few years (see further Desrosiers, below, pp. 139-44); and Professor Martin D. Snyder, past Director of the Classical Association of the Atlantic States' Latin Placement Service, has indicated that about 120 positions per year are advertised by the Service, but that only about 40 teacher applicants per year are registered.

Thus there can be little doubt that there is a general shortage of Latin teachers across the country and that in certain areas this shortage should be described as "critical." There is no single cure for the problem. However, it was apparent to many of the ACL survey respondents that there is a need to inform university faculty and their students about the prospects for entering the elementary- and secondary-school teaching profession. Many respondents suggested that PhD graduates without college and university teaching positions be encouraged to consider teaching at the secondary level, where salaries and career opportunities are often as good as (and sometimes better than) those offered by colleges and universities with increasingly difficult access to tenure and promotion. Others urged that the Classics profession devote attention to preparing teachers by 1) reactivating dormant teacher-training programs, 2) introducing new MAT programs, and 3) planning intensive programs for persons recently hired to teach Latin with minimal or sub-standard qualifications. The NEH-funded summer Latin Institutes at Westminster College and the University of Georgia (UGA) illustrate dramatically the need for this last type of program: 78 applications from teachers of other foreign languages, English, and social studies were received for the 20 available places in the 1984-85 Westminster Institutes and over 500 inquiries and 125 completed applications were received for the 25 positions in the 1986-87 ACL/UGA Institute (see Castro, below, pp. 31-42, and LaFleur and Anderson, below, pp. 43-62). There is clearly a very considerable need for these and a variety of other programs aimed at training more and better Latin teachers for American high-school classrooms: it is a need, and a challenge, to which college and university classicists must offer effective response.

For further information on Latin teacher placement, see the closing article and directory, below, pp. 145-57.

REFERENCES

1. Atelsekm, Frank J., and Irene L. Gomberg. *Newly Qualified Elementary and Secondary School Teachers, 1977-78 and 1978-79.*

Higher Education Panel Report 45. Washington, DC: American Council on Education, 1980.

2. Bridgman, A. "Rise in Foreign-Language Enrollments Spurs Teacher Shortage." *Education Week* 12 Sept. 1984: 1, 23.

3. Brod, Richard I., and Monica S. Devens. "Foreign Language Enrollments in U.S. Institutions of Higher Education—Fall 1983." *ADFL Bulletin* 16, ii (1985): 57-63.

4. Carnegie Task Force on Teaching as a Profession. *A Nation Prepared: Teachers for the 21st Century.* New York, NY: Carnegie Forum on Education and the Economy, 1986.

5. "Databank: Growth Years Ahead." *Education Week* 16 Apr. 1986: 20.

6. Empey, Donald W. "The Greatest Risk: Who Will Teach?" *Elementary School Journal* 86 (1984): 167-76.

7. Ferris, James, and Donald Winkler. "Teacher Compensation and the Supply of Teachers." *Elementary School Journal* 86 (1986): 389-403.

8. "Foreign Language Enrollments in Public Secondary Schools, Fall 1982." *Foreign Language Annals* 17 (1984): 611-23.

9. LaFleur, Richard A. "1984: Latin in the United States Twenty Years After the Fall." *Foreign Language Annals* 18 (1985): 341-47; rev. above, pp. 1-15.

10. Latimer, John F. *The Oxford Conference and Related Activities: A Report to The National Endowment for the Humanities.* Oxford, OH: ACL, 1968.

11. Masland, Susan W., and Robert T. Williams. "Teacher Surplus and Shortage: Getting Ready to Accept Responsibilities." *Journal of Teacher Education* 34, iv (1983): 6-9.

12. Metz, A. Stafford. *Teacher and School Administrator Supply and Demand.* Washington, DC: National Center for Education Statistics (USGPO), 1979.

13. National Center for Education Statistics. *Digest of Education Statistics.* Washington, DC: USGPO, 1960-85.

14. Olson, Lynn, and Blake Rodman. "Growing Need, Fewer Teachers: 'Everybody Is Out There Bidding'." *Education Week* 18 June 1986: 1, 11-13.

15. Phinney, Edward. "The Critical Shortage of Qualified Latin Teachers." *Prospects* 4 (1981): 1-2; rpt. in *Classical Outlook* 59 (1981): 10-11.

16. Rush, Gary S. "Corrective Measures in the Teacher Shortage: Consequences and Conclusions." *Education* 104 (1983-84): 34-37.

17. *Teacher Supply and Demand in Public Schools, 1981-82.* Washington, DC: National Education Association, 1983.

18. U.S. Department of Education. *The Condition of Education 1985 Edition.* Washington, DC: USGPO, 1985.

19. Wilhelm, Robert M. "Annual Report of the Director of the ACL Placement Service for Latin and Greek." In *American Classical League Annual Reports of Officers and Committee Chairmen.* Oxford, OH: ACL, 1978-86.

The Westminster Latin Institutes:
Prospects and Performance

A. Dwight Castro
Westminster College

For two six-week sessions in the summers of 1984 and 1985, 20 persons from across the country, all of them experienced teachers of various subjects (English, French, German, Spanish, history, social studies, religion), converged on the campus of Westminster College, a small, liberal arts school nestled in the Amish farmland of western Pennsylvania.[1] What induced them to forego summer vacations and to separate themselves from family and friends for the majority of these two summers was their desire to participate in the Westminster Latin Institutes, a pioneering program funded by a generous grant from the National Endowment for the Humanities (NEH) and designed to help alleviate the acute shortage of Latin teachers by providing experienced teachers of other subjects with the skills they would need to become qualified in Latin. In this paper I shall describe briefly the genesis, implementation, and outcomes of the Institutes, whose success has demonstrated their value as a model which others may imitate with profit.

By now the phenomenon of renewed interest in the study of Latin in American schools, following a long period of decline, is well established.[2] In fact, the change has been so dramatic in recent years that it has been deemed worthy of discussion, not just in professional journals,[3] but also in major newspapers and news magazines.[4] What a large segment of the American public in the 1980s has seemingly come to realize, albeit belatedly, is, on the one hand, the detrimental effect which the reduction or removal of Latin study from so many American schools during the 1960s and early 1970s had on the curriculum and on the basic skills (especially the verbal competence) of so many students, and, conversely, the educational benefits which the study of Latin can demonstrably convey.[5]

---

[1] Earlier versions of this paper were presented at the meeting of the American Philological Association in Toronto, Ontario, on December 29, 1984, and at the American Classical League (ACL) Institute in Austin, Texas, on June 21, 1985.

[2] See data in Wilhelm (10) and LaFleur (4), above.

[3] The most recent article is LaFleur (4).

[4] See, e.g., Bowen (1), LaFranchi (5), Stobart (7), Walsh (8), Woodall (11).

[5] See LaFleur (3), Brodie (2). In addition, a study by Patricia Davis Wiley (9) of

31

The resurgence of enrollments in Latin that has occurred over the past decade, however, has quickly outstripped the supply of available teachers. This was, of course, virtually inevitable. Not only were many qualified Latin teachers laid off, retired, or reassigned to teach other subjects during the period of decline in the 1960s and 1970s, but students who might have provided a new supply of teachers either did not receive the sort of exposure to Latin which would have stimulated their interest in teaching it, or else were simply discouraged by the uncertain long-term career prospects for teaching the language.[6] The shortage of qualified teachers has, in fact, now become the greatest barrier to an even greater resurgence of Latin instruction. After all, the good intentions of parents, school boards, and administrators to recover what was lost are meaningless if qualified teachers cannot be found.[7]

Complicating the current shortage of qualified Latin teachers is the further practical problem that, even where school boards and administrators now wish to reinstate Latin, the general student population in many areas of the United States—especially in the so-called "Rust Belt"—is currently declining, which means that schools are under financial pressure to freeze or reduce the size of teaching staffs, not increase them. Moreover, whenever Latin instruction is reinstated, it naturally begins with just elementary and intermediate levels, with a "wait and see" attitude towards instruction at advanced levels. This means that full-time positions

---

students at several state universities in Tennessee has shown that, while students who had studied *any* foreign language in high school achieved college grade point averages which were higher (at a statistically significant level) than those of students who had studied no foreign language at all, those who had studied Latin outperformed consistently those who had studied German, French, and Spanish.

[6] The dramatic decrease in the annual number of new teachers with certification in Latin is documented in Wilhelm (10); according to his statistics, detailed above pp. 17-30, the number of college and university students graduating with certification to teach Latin has not increased significantly in recent years, nor is it projected to do so.

[7] Statistics cited by Wilhelm (10) on the experience of the ACL Placement Service, the New England Latin Placement Service (see further Desrosiers, below, pp. 139-44), and the Classical Association of the Atlantic States (CAAS) Latin Placement Service in recent years dramatically point out the disparity, in all areas of the nation, between the number of schools seeking qualified Latin teachers and the number of available candidates. I would add that my experience as director of the CAAS Placement Service during 1985 suggested that the situation had, if anything, worsened: approximately 175 positions were listed that year, but only 45 candidates registered with the Service. In some cases additional candidates were located who had not registered with the Service, but in many instances positions either remained vacant or were filled with persons who were not adequately qualified to teach Latin.

in Latin alone are still not common, even if a school district is willing and able to hire new staff.

In light of all these circumstances, it seemed to us at Westminster College that meeting the need for qualified Latin teachers in the 1980s would require a different approach than simply increasing the number of graduates with teaching certificates in Latin from traditional BA undergraduate and MA and MAT graduate programs.[8] As long ago as 1981, when the signs of a resurgent interest in Latin on the part of secondary-school students, and the consequent potential teacher shortage, were just beginning to be noticed,[9] we had begun to discuss among ourselves in a very preliminary way the feasibility of offering some sort of summer program which would address this problem. At this point Marylee Houston, a 1978 alumna of Westminster who was then teaching Latin at the junior-senior high school in Greenville, Pennsylvania (a largely rural district in western Pennsylvania which, contrary to the prevailing trend of the 1970s, had not only maintained a full four-year Latin program, but had actually increased it), came to us to discuss her idea for coping with the immediate need for Latin teachers: retraining current teachers of other subjects, with the objective of enabling them to add Latin to their teaching certificates. This, she correctly reasoned, would appeal to school boards and administrators who wished to expand their curricular offerings to include Latin, but who could not find the money to hire new staff—assuming that they could even find fully qualified candidates.

Mrs. Houston's idea at once appealed to us. The practical problem was to develop a detailed proposal and, especially, to obtain financial support. After preliminary inquiries to several private foundations proved discouraging, we decided in the fall of 1982 to approach the National Endowment for the Humanities. When their initial reaction to our preliminary proposal was favorable, a detailed proposal for what we decided to call the "Westminster Latin Institutes," to consist of two sequential six-week sessions in the summers of 1984 and 1985, was submitted in June, 1983. In December of that same year the project was awarded the requested funding of nearly $100,000. The Institutes' stated purpose was "to enable teachers of English, modern languages, and other subjects, who already have some background in Latin, to broaden and deepen their knowledge of the Latin language

---

[8] The inability of these programs to meet the immediate need for qualified teachers is demonstrated above by Wilhelm (10).

[9] The first full report published on this subject (Phinney, 6) appeared in 1981.

and literature and of Roman culture, to the degree that they will be qualified to teach Latin in addition to their current fields." The competencies which were stated as the goals of each of the two sessions were based on the statement of "Proposed Standards for Secondary School Teachers of Latin" developed in 1968 (and still subscribed to) by the Pennsylvania Classical Association. Although (in response to the wishes of NEH) the certification process was not stressed in our final proposal, our advertising (which was developed with NEH approval) offered participants in the Institutes "assistance towards state certification" for any who wished it.

The grant proposal as finally drafted was submitted in the name of J. Hilton Turner, then Professor of Greek and Latin at Westminster College. As the junior member of the Classics faculty at Westminster, however, and one of the proposed faculty for the Institutes, I collaborated closely in designing the general program and had primary responsibility for writing several parts of the proposal. Further assistance was offered by Marylee Houston and by Dr. Rudolph Masciantonio, at that time Assistant Director of Foreign Language Education for the School District of Philadelphia.[10]

The faculty for the Institutes consisted of Professor Turner as Director, myself as Assistant Director, and an experienced and currently active high-school teacher, who was designated as a Master Teacher. This position of Master Teacher was filled for the 1984 session by Terrance DePasquale, a highly qualified and successful teacher in the Beaver Area (PA) High School, and for the 1985 session by Marylee Houston.[11]

Since our major funding was from NEH, we were to advertise the Institutes on a nationwide basis. Accordingly, we placed notices in all major foreign language periodicals (both classical and modern) and the major English periodicals. One paid advertisement was placed in *Education Week*. Notices were also sent to the National Education Association for inclusion in its regional publications, as well as to the Departments of Education of all 50 states for inclusion in their state newsletters. The last-mentioned notices were aimed not only at teachers, but also at school administrators,

[10] Dr. Turner currently holds the rank of Professor Emeritus of Greek and Latin (having retired from full-time teaching in August, 1984); Dr. Masciantonio is currently Director of Foreign Language Education for the School District of Philadelphia; and I am now the senior member of the Classics faculty at Westminster and the section head for Classics within the Department of Foreign Languages.

[11] Mrs. Houston was to have been the Master Teacher for both sessions but took maternity leave from the 1984 session.

whose support was considered vital if members of their staffs were to participate in the Institutes.

The response exceeded our most optimistic expectations: close to 300 persons from almost all parts of the country inquired about the Institutes between early February and May 1, 1984, the deadline for submitting completed applications. This proved to us that there was an even greater resurgence of interest in Latin and a need for teachers than had been previously supposed. In the end, we received 78 completed applications for the 20 available places in the Institutes.[12] We are convinced, however, that there would have been even more completed applications, except for the fact that, although our notices were sent out in late January, 1984, to the various media mentioned above, the *English Journal* and a few state education newsletters (notably those in New York and Ohio) were not able to publish information about the Institutes until late April—less than two weeks before the May 1 deadline for the submission of completed applications.[13]

In view of the large number of applications, we very early decided, as our first criterion for selecting participants, to reject the applications of those persons who had studied Latin for less than two years in college or four years in high school. The reason for this was our conviction that a reasonably complete prior exposure to the fundamentals of Latin would increase the likelihood that a person could attain, within the course of the two summer sessions of the Institutes, the sorts of competencies needed for certification in Latin. At the same time, however, our brochures describing the Institutes, which were sent to everyone who inquired about them, clearly advised that additional formal course work in Latin, beyond that offered by the Institutes, might well be needed by some participants in order to meet the specific requirements for certification in a given state.

At the other extreme, we also decided to reject applications from persons who had studied Latin so extensively at the college level (e.g., who had taken a major or a minor in Latin) that they did not, in our judgment, need both sessions of the Institutes to meet the minimum requirements for certification. Eleven persons from

[12] In addition to the 78 completed applications we received approximately 20 applications which had to be rejected outright for being incomplete.

[13] We did in fact receive almost 20 telephone calls just before and after May 1 from persons in various parts of New York asking for permission to submit applications after the deadline, due to the short notice which they had received. Those who called before May 1 were given one week to submit their completed applications, but those who called after that date had to be told, with regrets, that we already had more than enough qualified applicants.

this group of applicants, however, accepted our offer to be placed on a waiting list for the 1985 session, should someone from the original group of participants withdraw at the end of the 1984 session. As it turned out, only one person from the group who attended the 1984 session was unable to return for the 1985 session; consequently, 10 of the 11 persons on our waiting list could not be accommodated in the Institutes.[14]

Once the number of applicants had been narrowed by the elimination of the two extremes of prior training noted above, additional criteria were used to narrow the group to 20. The most important of these were the applicants' own statements of their interest in the Institutes and the supporting letters from school administrators. In the end, we selected only those persons who had either a certain or a very strong likelihood of at least partial employment as Latin teachers upon completion of the Institutes and the attainment of any necessary certification. In fact, we discovered a considerable number of applicants who had already begun to teach some Latin under an emergency certificate—or, in some instances, even without one. This was a further sign both of the desperate nature of the teacher shortage and of the desire of school districts to accommodate the demand for Latin instruction—as well as of the need for a program such as the Institutes to sharpen the Latin skills of those who were being asked and were willing to offer this instruction.[15]

Finally, since our program was being funded by a federal agency, and because we received applications from such a large number of states,[16] we were interested, once our other criteria had been met, in achieving at least some geographical spread among

[14] The one person of the original group of 20 who withdrew from the 1985 session did so only reluctantly, due to a last-minute family emergency which required her presence at home for most of the summer of 1985. However, by special arrangement, she was able to keep up with the work of the Institutes and was able to leave home long enough to come to Westminster at the end of the session to take the final examination (which she passed successfully). Thus, we may say that the Institutes actually accommodated 21 persons.

[15] Although a small number of our participants had always wanted to teach Latin, but had been discouraged from doing so by the factors cited earlier in this paper, most had never intended to teach the language, but either had been or were about to be pressed into service by desperate administrators who had discovered that they had some formal training in Latin, however slight and however many years earlier. This all too common phenomenon is also noted by Phinney (6), LaFleur (4), and Wilhelm (10).

[16] We received applications from persons in 37 states, plus the District of Columbia. The main gaps in the states were in the upper Midwest, the Rocky Mountains, and Alaska.

our participants. In the end, the 20 participants came from 11 states and the District of Columbia.[17]

Having discussed the genesis of our program, I shall now describe briefly the methods of instruction and the syllabus used for the two sessions of the Institutes. The reader will notice immediately that our approach was distinctly traditional, which suited not only our own inclinations but also the preferences of NEH. This did not mean, however, that we attempted to discourage innovation in the presentation of classroom instruction. Rather, we encouraged innovation built upon a solid base of traditional competencies.

The pace set for the Institutes was of necessity fairly intense. For both the 1984 and the 1985 sessions the participants met for about four hours of instruction, five days a week, for six weeks— more than the minimum time normally needed to earn the two course units (or seven semester hours) of undergraduate credit which the Institutes offered. The four hours each day were broken into three separate periods, each with a different type of instruction and content.

During the 1984 session each day began with one hour of reading (in Latin) and translation of assigned passages from two texts which we at Westminster College have found extremely useful at the intermediate level of instruction. One was M.G. Balme's *The Millionaire's Dinner Party* (Oxford University Press, 1973), which consists of adapted selections from the *Cena Trimalchionis* section of Petronius' *Satyricon*. This text presents, via the medium of continuous prose, a structured review of basic Latin syntax, beginning with simple structures and gradually working up to the more difficult ones. The second text was Ugo E. Paoli's *Ciceronis Filius* (photocopies of this out-of-print text were made with special permission of Professor Paoli's family), which skillfully presents not only Latin syntax and vocabulary, but also a fine introduction to Roman life of the first century BC, via the medium of a fictional story about the birth and growth of Cicero's son. Although it is not genuine Latin literature, Paoli uses a fine (although simplified) Ciceronian style of Latin. Both texts were well received by our participants. For this daily one-hour period the entire group of participants was divided into three smaller

---

[17] The 11 states represented were Arizona, Georgia, Hawaii, Maryland, Massachusetts, New Jersey, New York, North Carolina, Pennsylvania, Texas, and Virginia. There was one participant from the District of Columbia and one from each state, except Maryland (2), New York (2), and Pennsylvania (7).

sections of seven persons,[18] each supervised by one of the three faculty members on a rotating basis.

After a half-hour coffee break, the entire group met for a 90-minute plenary session, in which various aspects of Roman culture were presented (in English). The emphasis for 1984 was on Roman life and Greco-Roman mythology. After the first week, during which instruction was given by the faculty, the participants themselves presented during this period oral reports on assigned topics which they had researched. During these five weeks each participant presented two reports of about 30 minutes each, one on some aspect of Roman life or institutions and one on some aspect of mythology. Both the content and the method of presentation were to be geared to the type of students (i.e., elementary, junior-high, or senior-high) which the presenter expected to teach in his or her school. The faculty assisted each person individually with the development of a bibliography, the choice of a format for the presentation, and the duplication of materials.[19] The reports were carefully critiqued and graded by all three faculty.

Following a two-hour lunch break, the participants returned to their small groups for about 90 minutes of grammatical drill and Latin composition, using exercises from a traditional text, *A High School Course in Latin Composition*, by C.M. Baker and A.J. Inglis (out of print: photocopies were made by permission of the Macmillan Co.). During 1984 all instruction for this period was given by the faculty, again (as in the first period) on a rotating basis.

In addition to the three formal instructional periods just described, there were in 1984 several optional mid-afternoon meetings of two types: 1) morphological review for those who felt weak in this area, and 2) enrichment sessions which focused primarily on additional classroom resources and techniques.[20] Even though these mid-afternoon meetings were not required of participants, they were well attended and highly praised.

Two formal examinations were given, one at the mid-point and

[18] The 21st person in the group for each session was Sandra Hazen, a Westminster undergraduate (class of 1986) majoring in Latin, who also served as a student assistant for the Institutes.

[19] For these and all other presentations by participants, the presenter was encouraged to provide classroom-ready materials (e.g., lesson plans, bibliographies, student assignments, handouts, overhead transparencies) which all the participants could have for potential future use in their own classes. This was also done with faculty presentations of grammatical, literary, and ancillary cultural and historical material.

[20] Some of these enrichment sessions were led by Marianne Lorinchak of the Pittsburgh Public Schools, who has successfully developed numerous materials for classroom use, especially with disadvantaged and minority students.

one at the end of the session. These consisted of prepared and sight translation, simple Latin prose composition, and oral reading (in Latin) of a prepared prose passage. The mid-term was diagnostic in nature; the final was graded.

For the 1985 session the same three-period daily schedule was followed, with the first and third periods again consisting of small groups and the second being a plenary session. For the first period the syllabus in 1985 consisted of reading, discussion, and grammatical analysis of selections of genuine Latin literature from a variety of authors; the text used was D.P. Lockwood's two-volume *Survey of Classical Roman Literature* (University of Chicago Press, 1962). The second period again consisted of instruction in ancillary areas. In 1985 the topics were a survey of Roman history and the major authors of the Golden and Silver Ages. The instruction in Roman history was presented entirely by the faculty, but each author was presented via an oral report prepared, under the supervision of a member of the faculty, by one of the participants. The third period continued grammatical drill via Latin prose composition, again using Baker and Inglis, but this time the participants were asked to design and present, under the supervision of their group instructor, some of the lessons on grammatical structures.[21] The graded final examination was similar to the 1984 final, except that in 1985 the oral section consisted of the metrical reading of a prepared selection of lyric or epic poetry, and there was a brief essay question on Roman history.

As mentioned earlier, our primary objective for the Institutes was to provide 20 persons with the competencies they would need to teach Latin successfully, not just at the Latin I-II level (although, as a practical matter, this was our primary emphasis), but also at the III-IV level.[22] The secondary (and corollary) objective was to enable these persons, if they so desired and/or their schools required it, to obtain formal certification (either in Pennsylvania or their home states) to teach Latin in the public schools. Although we did not expect that all 21 of our participants[23] would attain both objectives at the end of the Institutes, we did hope that most of them would be able to start teaching Latin in the fall of 1985, at least on a part-time basis.[24] In this our hopes have been fulfilled. In

---

[21] The participants' presentations dealt primarily with the basic structures which teachers commonly encounter in teaching Latin I and II, and which the faculty had reviewed in some detail during the 1984 session.

[22] This was the reason for the readings from a wide variety of authors done during the first daily period of the 1985 session.

[23] I am including in this total the one alternate who joined the group in 1985.

[24] By this I do not mean that they would be only part-time teachers, but that as

addition to the nine persons who had already begun teaching Latin on an emergency basis before they attended the Institutes, our latest data show that nine more began teaching at least some Latin during the 1985-86 academic year, and two more during this current (1986-87) academic year. Thus, as of the writing of this article, only one person who attended the Institutes had not yet taught any Latin. Most of those who are teaching Latin are doing so in conjunction with the subjects which they had previously been teaching, and the Latin component forms one-half or less of their teaching load, but four persons report that they are now either fully or primarily teaching Latin.

The situation with regard to obtaining permanent certification in Latin for the participants in the Institutes has been complicated by the vastly disparate requirements of the various states in which they have sought such certification. At the end of the 1985 session of the Institutes four persons were immediately recommended for, and received, permanent Latin certification in Pennsylvania. During the 1985-86 academic year six more persons received Latin certification in Pennsylvania, and seven more received Latin certification in some other state. The remaining four persons either do not need state certification at this time (because they are teaching at private or parochial schools) or are continuing to work on the additional courses which their states require.[25]

In summary, the Westminster Latin Institutes have successfully demonstrated the feasibility of alleviating the current teacher shortage to some extent by providing a carefully selected group of experienced teachers with the sorts of competencies which they need to become properly qualified Latin teachers. The Institutes have also provided one practical model for accomplishing this objective in less than half the time that it normally takes an undergraduate student to complete a traditional Latin major with certification to teach. This model, to be sure, does have some limitations, primarily the fact that it is not designed for, nor would it probably work as successfully with, persons who have had no

---

full-time teachers, they would teach some Latin in addition to the other subject(s) which they were already teaching.

[25] The major problem which these teachers report is the difficulty in finding suitable Latin courses at colleges and universities near their homes which are both at an advanced level (i.e., higher than the elementary or intermediate level) and offered at times when full-time teachers can take them. Even large universities apparently do not regularly offer such courses in the evenings or during the summers. Classics departments across the country could, we believe, make a large contribution to dealing with the shortage of Latin teachers if they would offer their upper-level Latin courses on a more flexible schedule.

prior study of Latin. For those, however, who can meet the criteria which we used in selecting our participants, we believe it will work very well— as, indeed, it already has.

If, however, the shortage of Latin teachers is to be eliminated, there is obviously a need for more programs such as the Westminster Latin Institutes, and the ACL/University of Georgia Latin Institute described in the following essay, on numerous college and university campuses across the nation. Such a series of programs, even if run concurrently (as they should be), would not compete with, but would rather complement, each other. This will, of course, require substantial funding; nor can we expect, in light of ongoing federal budget reduction policies, that NEH will be able to provide it all. Only if private foundations and major universities become seriously committed to these sorts of projects can there be any real hope of meeting the needs of all the students who wish to avail themselves of the proven educational benefits of Latin study. But the time for action is now. If we lose the advantage which we currently enjoy with the American public, it may well be lost forever.

For further information on the Westminster Latin Institutes, write

Professor A. Dwight Castro
Department of Foreign Languages
Westminster College
New Wilmington, PA 16172

REFERENCES

1. Bowen, Ezra. "New Life for a Dead Language." *Time* 24 Dec. 1984: 61.
2. Brodie, Peter. "Why Study Latin?" *New York Times* 18 July 1984: A23.
3. LaFleur, Richard A. "Latin Students Score High on SAT and Achievement Tests." *Classical Journal* 76 (1981): 254.
4. ———. "1984: Latin in the United States Twenty Years After the Fall." *Foreign Language Annals* 18 (1985): 341-47; rev. above, pp. 1-15.
5. LaFranchi, Howard. "Teacher's Saga: Veni, Vidi, Vici." *Christian Science Monitor* 14 Dec. 1984: 1, 52.
6. Phinney, Edward. "The Critical Shortage of Qualified Latin Teachers." *Prospects* 4 (1981): 1-2; rpt. in *Classical Outlook* 59 (1981): 10-11.
7. Stobart, Janet. "Can 'Donaldus Anas,' a.k.a. Donald Duck, Take

the Drudgery Out of Latin?" *Christian Science Monitor* 25 June 1984: 7, 9.

8. Walsh, Elsa. "Dead Language Very Much Alive." *Washington Post* 22 July 1984: C1, 4.

9. Wiley, Patricia D. "High School Foreign Language Study and College Academic Performance." *Classical Outlook* 62 (1984-85): 33-36.

10. Wilhelm, Robert M. "The Shortage of Latin Teachers: Fact or Fiction?" *Classical Outlook* 62 (1985): 105-10; rev. above, pp. 17-30.

11. Woodall, Martha. "The Fall and Rise of Latin." *Philadelphia Inquirer* 29 Apr. 1984: B1, 8.

Meeting the Need for Latin Teachers: The American Classical League/ University of Georgia NEH Latin Institute

Richard A. LaFleur
James C. Anderson, Jr.
University of Georgia

I. PROGRAM DESCRIPTION

A. *The Proposal and Its Objectives*

After declining nearly 80% between 1962 and 1976, high-school Latin enrollments have been steadily rising for the past decade.[1] A disturbing consequence of this otherwise felicitous trend has been the development of a serious shortage of fully qualified Latin teachers. As a result, plans for new or expanded programs have sometimes been curtailed or even abandoned; in numerous instances teachers certified in other areas but lacking certification in Latin have been assigned to teach the language. The National Latin Institute here described, funded by the National Endowment for the Humanities (NEH) and co-sponsored by the University of Georgia (UGA) and the American Classical League (ACL), was designed as a response to this critical problem, to strengthen Latin instruction in America's secondary schools and to help relieve the shortage of certified Latin teachers. Dr. Richard A. LaFleur, President of the ACL during 1984-86 and Professor and Head of Classics at Georgia, and Dr. James C. Anderson, Jr., Associate Professor of Classics at Georgia, submitted an initial prospectus to the Endowment's Division of Education Programs in September, 1984; with the generous assistance and counsel of Dr.

[1] Abbreviated versions of this paper were presented in 1986 by Professors LaFleur and Anderson at the annual meeting of the Foreign Language Association of Georgia (September, Athens, GA) and by Professor LaFleur at meetings of the Southern Conference on Language Teaching and the Florida Foreign Language Association (October, Orlando, FL), the Indiana Foreign Language Teachers Association and Indiana Classical Conference (October, Indianapolis, IN), and the American Philological Association (December, San Antonio, TX); updates will be presented in 1987, by Professor Anderson, at the annual meeting of the Classical Association of the Middle West and South (April, Boulder, CO), and, by Professor LaFleur, at the American Classical League Institute (June, Washington, DC); a less detailed preliminary report appeared in the December/January, 1986-87, *Classical Outlook* (LaFleur and Anderson, 10).

Stephanie Quinn Katz, the NEH Program Officer assigned to the project, the final proposal was submitted in December, 1984. With only minimal program and budgetary revision required, the project was awarded, in July of 1985, a grant of $249,860 toward a total budget of nearly $400,000, the remainder contributed as cost-sharing by the University System of Georgia, the University of Georgia, the American Classical League, and a number of Latin textbook publishers, as detailed below. The present study is meant to provide both a report on the progress of the Institute during its first year and a detailed description that might serve as a model for university Classics departments seeking to develop similar programs for the training of Latin teachers.

The Institute consists of two intensive five-week summer sessions, held on the UGA campus (Athens, GA), July 7-August 8, 1986, and June 26-July 31, 1987, with a variety of continuation and follow-up activities scheduled for the 1986-87 and 1987-88 academic years while the participants are teaching in their home schools. Participants in the Institute receive intensive instruction in the language, from the beginning into the advanced level, and in aspects of the civilization, history, and literature of the Romans centering on the theme, "From Republic to Empire."

Participants satisfactorily completing this two-year program should have attained at least the minimum language proficiency necessary for teaching Latin I-IV at the secondary level, an understanding of several major aspects of Roman society, and a firm grasp of the complex of ideas and issues involved in the collapse of the Roman Republic and the emergence of the Principate during the first century BC, one of the most crucial periods in the history of Roman—and Western—civilization. In addition, through a series of lectures, workshops, and exhibits, as well as the actual use of texts suitable for employment in the high-school classroom, participants will become broadly familiar with methods and materials for teaching Latin in the schools.

B. *Publicity*

The program was widely publicized through a variety of media, beginning in July, 1985, and reached an estimated minimum of 200,000 educators. Full-page paid advertisements were placed in the October *Phi Delta Kappan* (circulation 145,473), the October *Foreign Language Annals* (circulation 9,000), the October-November and December-January *Classical Outlook* (circulation 3,400), and the October Bolchazy-Carducci Publishers catalog (circulation 15,000). The same full-page camera-ready notices were mailed in July to more than 60 Classics, foreign language, and other educational journals and newsletters with the request that they be published at no cost; as a result, full-page ads or shorter announcements appeared in more than 30 of those publications, including such widely circulated periodicals as the *National Association of Secondary School Principals NewsLeader* (circulation 36,000). Approximately 9,000 descriptive fliers were distributed during the fall to all ACL members, all state foreign language coordinators, about 800 Classics and foreign language departments, and to numerous other educators and administrators around the country. Professor LaFleur gave a number of interviews to persons from the media, resulting in mention of the project in at least 15 news releases, and delivered presentations on the Latin teacher shortage and the NEH Institute during 1985-86 at meetings of the Southern Conference on Language Teaching (October 11), the Classical Association of Florida/Florida Foreign Language Association (October 18), the Classical Association of Virginia (November 2), the American Philological Association (December 28), and the Alabama Classical Association/Alabama Association of Foreign Language Teachers (February 8). Fliers and other information on the Institute were distributed at each of these meetings.

C. *Eligibility, Applications, and Applicant Selection*

Eligible to apply were secondary-school teachers from across the country who were currently teaching Latin or were firmly committed, preferably under contract, to do so beginning in either 1986 or 1987, and whose formal training in the language was insufficient for certification. It was announced to all applicants that some preference would be given to teachers only recently assigned to teach Latin and to applicants whose primary teaching field was another foreign language or English, and that, insofar as practicable, attention would be given to insuring a national geographical distribution.

Requests for information and application materials began arriving in July, 1985, and by the April 1, 1986, deadline more than 500 inquiries had been received. Application packets containing a cover letter, a detailed program description, application, essay, and recommendation forms, and full instructions were mailed to over 400 persons; 170 persons from 38 states initiated the application process and 125 had completed their application by the April 1 deadline.[2]

_____

[2] In addition to the 125 applications fully completed by April 1, 24 were substantially complete by the deadline (including 4 fully complete by April 4); the

After a meticulous pre-screening procedure that continued from January through early April, 1986, the applicant selection committee met for a full-day session on April 9. Applicants eliminated included those who 1) had no previous formal training in Latin, 2) had the equivalent of a minor or major in Latin, or certification in Latin, and thus were overqualified, 3) had only average or below average academic credentials, especially in language courses, or 4) demonstrated insufficient evidence that they would be employed in a secondary-school Latin teaching position in 1986 or 1987. Twenty-five participants and 11 alternates[3] were selected by the committee, which consisted of Professors LaFleur and Anderson, the program's Project Director and Assistant Director, Ms. Lynne Bell McClendon of North Springs High School (Atlanta), the program's Master Teacher, Dr. William K. Jackson, of UGA's Office of Instructional Development, and Dr. Maureen O'Donnell of W. T. Woodson High School (Fairfax, VA), representative of the American Classical League. Letters were sent to all successful candidates, alternates, and unsuccessful candidates by April 15. All the alternates and unsuccessful candidates were encouraged to affiliate with ACL if they were not already members, and to apply for the League's McKinlay Scholarship, which can be used toward costs of tuition for summer school Latin courses at any accredited college or university; several were referred to other sources for assistance with certification, teaching materials, and other needs.

All 25 of the first-ranked applicants invited to participate in the Institute accepted the invitation, so there was no recourse to the 1986 alternates. The participants include: Karl Cason Beason (SC), Sister Mary Juliann Bilow (OH), Edith J. Black (GA), Martha Anne Boseski (SC), Susan M. Bradley (MD), Susan A. Burden (AR), Mary Darden Camp (GA), Sister Mary Susan Emmerich (MO), Patricia Falkenberry (CO), Muriel Ann Garcia (CA), Sister Elinor Hartman (MD), Antonia E. Howington (FL), Virginia Kannengiesser (PA), Karen McAferty (FL), Kathleen McGonigle (MA), Cornelius W. Nett (LA), Lorraine Purdy (VA), Nancy Reed (KY), Philip R. Sharpe (AL),[4] Theresa L. Shugart (TX), Patricia Silver (MD), Joseph

---

remaining 21 applications were substantially incomplete and were consequently disqualified.

[3] The 11 alternates included 6 with somewhat more extensive Latin training who might enter the program in 1987, in case any of the 1986 participants were not able to continue.

[3] Mr. Sharpe moved from Alabama to Georgia after the Institute's 1986 Summer Session to take up a Latin position in Atlanta which came to his attention during

Vasturia (PA), Marsha W. Walper (FL), Diane Whitmore (ME), and Elizabeth Zaboly (OH). The participants had been teaching Latin at levels ranging from Latin I through Latin IV for an average of two years and had themselves taken an average total of only four Latin courses in high school and college; three are teaching Latin for the first time in 1986-87; and one, after having taught Latin for four years during 1965-69, will begin teaching the language again in 1987-88.[5]

D. *Course Credit and Certification*

Participants successfully completing the work required in the Institute will receive 35 quarter-hours of non-resident credit from the University of Georgia, including 30 hours in Latin language and literature and 5 graduate hours in Roman Civilization.[6] Since certification requirements vary widely from state to state and may involve further work in the teaching field as well as in language education and other professional education courses, prospective applicants were advised to consult with their local certification officials; it is expected, however, that certification boards in most states will offer significant credit toward certification for work completed in the Institute. All participants will take the Georgia Teacher Certification Test in Latin at the end of the Institute as one measure of their progress toward certification.

E. *Funding and Participant Support*

Participants receive full waiver of tuition, all textbooks, room, board (three meals daily, Monday-Friday), and a $1,000 stipend for each of the two five-week summer sessions; transportation costs averaging $310 for each summer session and for the Mid-Year and Post-Institute Conferences (February 19-21 and December 3-5,

---

the Session, via an announcement from the Georgia Classical Association's Latin Teacher Placement Service.

[5] The 25 participants represent 17 states; all hold the bachelor's degree (12 of them in English, 11 in foreign languages, the others in social sciences), and several have Masters degrees; ages at the time of application ranged from 25 to 59; the majority (16) have taught (all subjects—not Latin) from 1-5 years, while 4 have taught from 16-25 years; 18 teach in public schools, 7 in private schools, all at the secondary level; 9 have academic responsibilities in addition to their teaching, including 6 who are department heads; 24 are teaching Latin during 1986-87 and the other, as indicated above, is firmly assigned to teach Latin beginning in 1987–88; participants are teaching a large variety of other subjects (art, religion, journalism, etc.), with the majority, however, in English (10) and/or modern foreign languages (15).

[6] All participants separately applied and were admitted in a "Post-baccalaureate" status to the UGA Graduate School and were registered in the University's Summer Session prior to their arrival on campus.

1987) are also provided. The participants' home schools or school districts are required to contribute $200 toward the costs of the stipends for each summer session, as well as the costs of substitute teachers and released time enabling the participants' attendance at the Mid-Year and Post-Institute Conferences; for those participants traveling greater distances, the local institutions are in most instances also providing supplemental travel funding.

The very generous financial support awarded the project is worthy of special note. The most substantial contribution, of course, is that of the National Endowment for the Humanities, whose grant of nearly $250,000 largely provided staff salaries, the participants' allowances for stipends, transportation, room and board, and a portion of the textbook costs, as well as honoraria and travel expenses for visiting lecturers, printing, mailing, and other miscellaneous expenses.

The University of Georgia's cost-sharing contribution, however, is also a very sizable one, amounting to over $30,000 in salaries, travel, computer time, and other costs. In addition, as further detailed below, much of the participants' work in the Institute has been organized within the framework of specially designed University credit courses as a means of facilitating the participants' progress toward certification in their home states. Under NEH guidelines, there may be no charges for tuition in any Institute budget nor any waiver of such charges specifically included as part of the sponsoring institution's cost-sharing. Georgia state regulations, however, require that tuition be paid for all persons enrolled for credit in any University System institution. Accordingly, in addition to the University's cost-sharing noted above, and as a demonstration of commitment to the purposes of the Institute, the Board of Regents of the University System of Georgia authorized an extraordinary waiver of the out-of-state tuition differential for the 23 out-of-state participants in the Institute, amounting to more than $45,000, and the University of Georgia agreed to pay the remaining in-state tuition costs of over $35,000.

Others supporting the project include 1) the American Classical League, which has committed funds and services totalling nearly $8,000; 2) the participants' home institutions, which are providing approximately $20,000 toward stipends, released time, and travel, as indicated above; and 3) several publishers, who have contributed textbooks and services valued at approximately $8,000.[7]

---

[7] Publishers who provided textbooks at no cost for the participants' coursework include: Allyn and Bacon, Longman, Macmillan, Olivia and Hill, and Yale

F. *Staff*

In addition to the three principal faculty members, Dr. LaFleur, Dr. Anderson, and Ms. McClendon, the staff includes an Administrative Assistant (Ms. Mary Wells Ricks, Assistant Editor of the *Classical Outlook*) and a Student Assistant and Tutor (Mr. John Nicholson, an experienced high-school teacher and 1986 University of Georgia MA graduate, currently enrolled in the doctoral program in Classics at the University of North Carolina).

Presentations by 18 Visiting Faculty supplement the experiences of participants during the two summer sessions and the Mid-Year Conference; the Visiting Faculty include: Richard Beaton (Griffin High School, Griffin, GA), Herbert W. Benario (Emory University), Gerald R. Culley (University of Delaware), John A. Dutra (Miami University), Jane Hall (Alexandria, VA), Judith P. Hallett (University of Maryland), George W. Houston (University of North Carolina), Jared S. Klein (UGA), Bobby W. LaBouve (Texas Education Agency), Gilbert W. Lawall (University of Massachusetts), Agnes K. Michels (Duke University), M. Gwyn Morgan (University of Texas), Naomi J. Norman (UGA), Michael C. J. Putnam (Brown University), Kenneth J. Reckford (University of North Carolina), Robert J. Rowland (University of Maryland), Harry C. Rutledge (University of Tennessee), and Judith Lynn Sebesta (University of South Dakota).

University Press. Publishers who provided discounted texts include: Harvard University Press, Longman, Oxford University Press, and the University of Oklahoma Press. Publishers contributing materials for the Institute's Text and Materials Exhibit include: Allyn and Bacon, Applause Learning Resources, Aspioti-Elka Co., Barnes and Noble, Bolchazy-Carducci, Bristol Classical Press, Bryn Mawr Latin Commentaries, Budek, Cambridge University Press, Caratzas Brothers, Cobblestone, College Press, F. A. Davis, Educational Audio-Visuals Inc., Edwards Brothers, Fordham University Press, Gardnor House, Gessler Educational Software, G.I.A. Publications, Harcourt Brace Jovanovich, Harvard University Press, D.C. Heath, Humanities Press, Independent School Press, International Film Bureau, Longman, Microforms Inc., National Textbook, NECN Publications, Jeffrey Norton, Olivia and Hill, Oxford University Press, Peter Pauper Press, Phillips Exeter Academy Press, Pompeiana Inc., Pontifical Institute for Medieval Studies, Reading Laboratories Inc., Southern Illinois University Press, B. G. Teubner, University of Alabama Press, University of Arizona Press, University of Michigan Press, University of North Carolina Press, University of Oklahoma Press, University of Pittsburgh Press, University of Texas Press, University of Vermont Press, Wayne State University Press, and Yale University Press. In addition, both Cambridge and Longman sent representatives to the Institute and provided funding for receptions. To these publishers, as well as to the many others who have supported the Institute in a variety of ways (including most especially the University of Georgia administration and its Office of Instructional Development and, of course, the officers and staff of the American Classical League), the Institute's faculty, staff, and participants are abundantly grateful.

II. INSTITUTE ACTIVITIES

A. *Preliminary Activities*

Participants in the Latin Institute began their work even before the first Summer Session opened in July. A list of readings, the necessary textbooks, and a tentative daily calendar for the Session, were all mailed to the participants on May 15. Preliminary readings were required in Roman history and civilization in order to insure the background necessary to a full appreciation of the cultural material to be explored during the summer. These readings included the full texts of Henry C. Boren's *Roman Society* (Boren, 1), one of the best available textbooks on Roman history and culture, and Jerome Carcopino's *Daily Life in Ancient Rome* (2), a standard text providing an examination of Roman daily life, manners, customs, beliefs, and attitudes. In addition, in preparation for the first day of the Summer Session, participants were required to read and study the Preface, Introduction, and first chapter of Frederic M. Wheelock's *Latin* (18) as well as the Teacher's Handbook for Lawall and Tafe, *Ecce Romani I: Meeting the Family* (11).

B. *The 1986 Summer Session*

The work of the first Summer Session (which began on Monday, July 7, following a successful registration and orientation session and a welcoming reception held during the weekend of July 5–6), focused upon intensive study of the Latin language as well as on important aspects of Roman culture, especially Roman social history and daily life of the late Republican and early Imperial periods. The cultural material (which concentrated on four topics: Roman Social Relations, Roman Religion, the Romans at Work, and the Romans at Leisure) was examined through lectures, outside research and reports prepared by the participants, and Latin readings in both Wheelock and *Ecce Romani*. Participants were enrolled in three Latin courses specially designed for the Institute, each meeting two hours daily and each carrying five quarter-hours of credit. Dr. Anderson had primary responsibility for LAT 198G and 199G (the Wheelock courses), with Dr. LaFleur assisting; Dr. LaFleur had primary responsibility for LAT 200G (the *Ecce Romani* course), with Dr. Anderson assisting.

1. *Formal Latin Instruction*

Frederic Wheelock's *Latin* was the primary textbook in the sequential LAT 198G and 199G courses; this book, the most widely used college-level Latin text in the United States, is particularly well suited to adult learners and to the intensive approach employed in the Institute. Norma Goldman and Ladislas Szymanski's *English Grammar for Students of Latin* (6) served as a supplementary text focusing upon similarities and differences between English and Latin grammar (LaFleur, 9). These two courses comprehensively surveyed the following topics: origins of the Latin language, its place in the Indo-European language family, and its relationship to English; the Roman alphabet; pronunciation and the importance of oral-aural exercises in the learning and teaching of Latin; all basic morphology and syntax; a considerable working vocabulary together with studies in English etymology; and techniques in reading, comprehension, and translation of Latin. Attention was given to the relationship between Latin and English and the importance of Latin for gaining an improved knowledge of English vocabulary, syntax, and related language skills. Daily activities included extensive grammar and vocabulary drill, oral-aural practice, prepared translations (both Latin to English and English to Latin), sight reading for comprehension, and other interactive exercises, with explicit attention to the rationale and methodology of applications in the secondary-school Latin I and II classroom. In addition, participants were required to complete a number of lessons in the PLATO program of computer-assisted instruction in Latin (see Scanlan, 15).

A variety of different approaches to learning and teaching Latin were introduced, including the traditional grammar/translation approach in Wheelock, and the less highly structured, more inductive "grammar in context" method employed in the new North American edition of *Ecce Romani* (Lawall and Tafe, 11, and see also Palma, 13), which served as the principal text for LAT 200G. Via the readings in *Ecce Romani*, material learned in Wheelock, including morphology and syntax, was reinforced, and additional material, especially vocabulary, was encountered; most importantly, further experience with reading, comprehension, oral-aural exercises, and translation was acquired through readings (often at sight) that centered upon the day-to-day activities of a late first-century AD Roman family. Cultural topics examined in the *Ecce Romani* readers included the Roman family, Roman dress, dining, bathing, and other daily routines; slavery; travel; graffiti; domestic and public architecture; the circus, the arena, and other entertainments; crafts, technology, and commerce; city versus country life; education; weddings, funerals, and other ceremonies; religion and mythology; farming and soldiering; and Roman politics.

2. Roman Culture Lecture Series

Four of the Visiting Faculty during the 1986 Summer Session presented a series of lectures that supplemented and reinforced the participants' study of Roman culture. Professor Judith P. Hallett lectured on Roman Social Relations, a topic embracing the Roman class system, slavery, the Roman family and kinship structures, and especially the role of women, thus providing added dimension to the treatment of the family in *Ecce Romani*. Professor Agnes Michels directed a session on Roman Religion as one of the most dynamic forces in Roman society. Presentations on the Romans at Work and the Romans at Leisure were made by, respectively, Professor George W. Houston and Professor M. Gwyn Morgan: Professor Houston discussed traditional Roman occupations and, in particular, explored Rome's economy through an examination of her trade, crafts, and technology; Professor Morgan lectured and led a discussion on the modes of Roman entertainment, including games and sports, theatrical performances, the development of public baths as social clubs and gathering places, and especially the Roman fascination with blood sports. In the aggregate, these four lectures, together with outside readings assigned for each, served to provide each participant with a fuller awareness of the major characteristics of Roman society and a vivid sense of what it was like to be a Roman. In addition, Professor Jared Klein spoke on the relationship of Latin to English and their place in the Indo-European language family; and Professor Naomi Norman gave a presentation on archaeological techniques and the UGA Excavations at Carthage. These lectures were often supplemented by readings, comments, and slide presentations provided by Professors Anderson and LaFleur.

3. Paedagogy and Professional Topics Sessions

Each week a session on a variety of paedagogical and professional topics appropriate to the teaching of Latin was moderated and supplemented by Ms. McClendon, the Institute's Master Teacher, assisted by Dr. LaFleur. Each session centered on presentations made by representatives of the American Classical League, including Professor Judith Lynn Sebesta, ACL Vice President and chair of the Latin Methodology and Basic Skills Committee; Dr. Richard Beaton, member of the Board of Directors of the National Junior Classical League; Ms. Jane Hall, ACL Secretary and chair of the National Latin Exam Committee; Professor Jack Dutra, Director of the ACL's Teaching Materials and Resource Center; and Mr. Bobby LaBouve, chairman of the

League's National Committee for Latin and Greek. These sessions systematically introduced participants to traditional and innovative methodologies and resources for teaching Latin and managing a successful Latin program at the secondary-school level. Representatives from two publishers also gave presentations that focused on methods and materials: Professor Edward Phinney (University of Massachusetts at Amherst) on the Cambridge Latin Course, and Ms. Thalia Pantelidis (Maury High School, Norfolk, VA) on Longman's *Ecce Romani* series.

4. *Exhibits and Social Activities*

Optional late afternoon and evening activities during the 1986 Summer Session included an exhibit from the ACL's Teaching Materials and Resource Center; an extensive publishers' exhibit of textbooks and classroom materials; an exhibit of rare Greek and Latin texts from the University of Georgia Libraries, directed by Ms. Mary Ellen Brooks; and more than a dozen receptions and dinners, arranged for the most part in connection with the visits of guest speakers and providing ample opportunity for continued discussion with the visitors and for socializing generally.[8]

All participants successfully completed the three formal Latin courses into which most of the Session's language work was organized. The very extensive material in Wheelock Chapters 1-40 and volumes 1-4 of the *Ecce Romani* series was covered quite thoroughly, along with a considerable amount of ancillary material. Grammar was treated exhaustively; oral-aural skills and expressive reading were given exceptional emphasis; considerable time was devoted to both prepared and unseen reading and translation exercises; all participants gained significant experience with textbook evaluation; all worked with the PLATO program of computer-assisted instruction in Latin; several prepared and presented to the group a variety of classroom materials suitable for use in the high-school Latin classroom. The days (and the nights) were long and the work was very intensive; nonetheless, nearly all the participants earned A's in all three courses (all grades were A's in both LAT 198G and LAT 200G, and there were only 4 B's in LAT 199G).

[8] A reception was generously sponsored, as part of a guided tour of the Georgia Museum of Art, by the office of the University's Vice President for Academic Affairs, Dr. M. Louise McBee; a party for both the Institute's and the Classics Department's faculty, staff, and students was hosted by Dr. and Mrs. LaFleur at their home; and a very gracious reception was given by University President and Mrs. Henry King Stanford at the President's home.

Despite differences of personality and temperament that must be expected in a group of adults from varied backgrounds, ranging in age from mid-20s to late 50s, and all of them removed from more comfortable and familiar surroundings to the close quarters of a college dormitory setting, the participants functioned in general as a happy (though sometimes harried) and congenial community of teacher-students sharing common interests and common goals. The social experience, in short, was about as positive as could be expected—more so, in fact, than might have been expected—not least due to the extraordinary efforts of the Institute staff, Ms. Ricks in particular.

C. 1986–87 Continuation Activities

As a means of maintaining their skills in Latin, enriching their knowledge of Roman history, and acquiring the basic familiarity with classical mythology generally expected of high-school Latin teachers, participants are continuing their work during academic year 1986-87, while back in their home schools, via four continuation activities: 1) completion of a correspondence course in Intermediate Latin; 2) independent reading of the text *Classical Mythology* by Morford and Lenardon (12); 3) participation in a Mid-Year Conference held on the UGA campus, February 19-21, 1987; and 4) contact with a Mentor, an experienced Latinist in or near the participant's hometown, during the academic year.[9]

1. The Latin 203 Correspondence Course

Participants are at work throughout academic 1986-87 on a correspondence course in Intermediate Latin (LAT 203), which involves extensive readings in Hammond and Amory, *Aeneas to Augustus* (7), as well as Colby, *Review Latin Grammar* (3), and Crawford, *The Roman Republic* (4). Dr. Anderson serves as instructor for this course, which he designed and which is administered through the Office of Independent Study of the Georgia Center for Continuing Education; participants receive five quarter-hours of credit upon successful completion of the 14 written assignments and the final examination that constitute the work of the course. While one goal of this course is to maintain and enhance the command of Latin gained during the preceding summer, an equal purpose is to provide each participant with a more detailed knowledge of the history of Rome during the Republic and her expansion and development from earliest times

---

[9] An orientation session for these activities was held, and the necessary textbooks were distributed, during the closing week of the 1986 Summer Session.

down to the late Republic. This is accomplished in part by the structure of the *Aeneas to Augustus* text, in which Latin passages (of increasing complexity) from classical and post-classical authors are arranged to provide a chronological history of Regal and Republican Rome and are provided with historical commentaries in English to underline significant events and developments. The supplementary texts by Colby and Crawford reinforce, respectively, the participants' review of the Latin language and their skills in analysis of political and social developments in the history of Rome. Thus, by the time they return for the second Summer Session, participants should be well prepared for a rigorous study of Rome's metamorphosis from Republic to Empire, and at the same time be ready to read and appreciate the major authors of that period in the original Latin. Such an opportunity for language learning within the context of a detailed intellectual consideration of a pivotal period in the history of Western culture is rare and should provide a unique stimulus to the learning of Latin and Roman history for the Institute's participants.

2. Independent Reading in Classical Mythology

In addition to the LAT 203 course, participants are required to read the textbook *Classical Mythology*, by Morford and Lenardon (12), which provides not only a thoroughgoing survey of the principal Greek and Roman myths, extensive excerpts from the ancient sources, and some interpretative analysis, but also material on the use of classical myth in later literature, music, ballet, art, and film, and an extensive bibliography that includes resources appropriate to the secondary-school classroom. This independent reading project is designed to insure that participants are conversant with those myths that will be encountered 1) directly or by allusion in the Latin literature read during the second Summer Session, and 2) in the natural course of teaching Latin I-IV in the schools. An examination on the principal characters and actions, and the major literary sources, of the most important classical myths will be administered during the 1987 Summer Session.

3. Mid-Year Conference

Participants returned to the University of Georgia, February 19-21, 1987, for a Mid-Year Conference, at which their progress in teaching and independent study was assessed, assistance for LAT 203 was provided, Professor Herbert W. Benario (Emory University) surveyed the collapse of Republican political institutions in a presentation titled *"Non Mos, Non Ius,"* and Professor Harry C. Rutledge (University of Tennessee) lectured and led a discussion on the topic "From Republic to Empire: Roman Myths and Mythmakers." Professor Rutledge's presentation was both literary and historical in its concerns, and considered in particular the uses of myth made by writers at work during Augustus' rise to power and the emergence of the principate. For those participants then involved in the teaching of Latin in their schools (all but one), an evaluation of applications of the previous summer's work to their teaching during 1986-87, together with an assessment of the Mentor program and of any anticipated special needs for the 1987 Summer Session, was undertaken in discussion with the Institute faculty.

4. Mentor Program

To assist them with carrying what they have learned into their own Latin classrooms during academic year 1986-87, all of the participants have been assigned local resource persons, or "Mentors." These Mentors, identified by the Institute Director, are experienced high-school or college Latin teachers, drawn largely from the membership of the American Classical League, who live in or near the participants' hometowns and who have offered their support on a voluntary basis.[10] Participants have been encouraged to call upon these Mentors, within reasonable limits, for classroom visits, suggestions and criticism, guidance regarding classroom activities and organization, materials, methods, and so forth; the Mentors themselves have been encouraged to call upon the Institute Director for assistance and asked to submit a brief report of their activities at the end of the academic year and, whenever possible, to continue in the role of Mentor during 1987-88.

D. The 1987 Summer Session

The participants' work during the second Summer Session (June 26-July 31, 1987) provides the intellectual climax of the Institute with its focus upon the theme, "From Republic to Empire." The intellectual demands of this Session's work are considerable, but the participants have been well prepared through their studies over the preceding months. As in the 1986 Summer Session, in order to facilitate their progress toward certi-

---

[10] In response to a call for Mentors distributed via an ACL mailing to about 6,100 Latin and Classics teachers in August, 1985, and to notices published in the March-April and May-June, 1986, issues of the *Classical Outlook*, a total of 50 persons in 20 states and the District of Columbia volunteered to serve in this capacity. Mentors had been identified from that pool of volunteers and from other sources for all 25 participants by the fall of 1986.

fication in their home states, participants are enrolled in three specially designed courses, for 15 quarter-hours credit, each meeting two hours daily, including advanced courses in Latin prose and verse and a Roman Civilization course that carries graduate seminar credit for all participants. While one important purpose of the two Latin courses is to improve the linguistic and translation skills acquired by the participants during the 1986 Summer Session and over the intervening academic year, both courses are also designed to complement the content of the Roman Civilization seminar. The combined work of these three courses provides the participants the opportunity to study in considerable depth one crucial period of Roman history, a period also central to the development of Roman literature and culture.

1. Seminar on the Rise of Augustus

The seminar on Roman Civilization (CLC 802), directed by Dr. Anderson, concentrates its investigation on the collapse of the Roman Republic and the establishment of the Empire under Augustus. While considering major developments from the Gracchan revolution into the early first century AD, the seminar examines in particular the years from 70 to 12 BC, i.e., from the rise to power of Pompey the Great to the final consolidation of Augustus' principate with his assumption of the position of pontifex maximus. During that period of 58 years the entire Roman system of government was altered, many of the most enduring works of Roman literature and art were created, the city of Rome was all but entirely rebuilt, Italy and the Mediterranean world suffered two destructive civil wars yet emerged more powerful than before, and the lives of all those peoples under Roman sway were significantly changed. In CLC 802, participants immerse themselves in this period of crisis. They read one of the most important and most controversial historical studies of the period ever written—*The Roman Revolution* by Sir Ronald Syme (16)—and consider its presentation of the period and Syme's brilliant but much-debated analysis of Rome's political metamorphosis during those years. H. T. Rowell's excellent study, *Rome in the Augustan Age* (14), is read as a supplementary text, for coverage of related topics only briefly considered by Syme (e.g., the rebuilding of the city). Study of Syme's book, along with Vergil's *Aeneid* in translation, should provoke considerable discussion and debate among participants already well versed in the earlier history and culture of Rome; in addition, participants are reading at the same time, in their Latin courses, the primary ancient sources for the late Republican/early Imperial period. Written essays, some cast in the form of Roman *suasoriae* and *controversiae*, are required as part of the weekly work in this course, with a final comprehensive essay submitted after the conclusion of the Session. Individual oral reports on specific topics may also be required.

2. Advanced Readings in Latin Prose and Verse

In the summer's advanced Latin courses, as in the seminar, work is centered on the theme "From Republic to Empire." While studying Syme's and Rowell's historical treatments and discussing their interpretations in depth, participants read simultaneously the primary literary sources, both prose and poetry, for the period 70-12 BC in the original Latin; each Latin course is organized, and the readings selected, for this purpose. In the prose course (Lat 420), directed by Professor Anderson, participants read substantial selections from the works of the two central figures—literary as well as political—of the last years of the Roman Republic, Caesar and Cicero. In addition, selections from the contemporary historians Sallust and Livy, and the *Res Gestae* of Augustus are read. In this course, while participants encounter these authors and come to understand them through their own words and in their own language, they also can consider, through the eyes of actual participants, such crucial events of the period as the conspiracy of Catiline, in the reports of both Cicero and Sallust, the conquest of Gaul as described by Caesar and commented upon by Cicero, and a variety of other significant events. The principal texts for the course are Ullman, et al., *Latin for Americans* (17), second and third books, two volumes from one of the Latin textbook series most widely adopted in this country. All the selections of Latin prose that are read—speeches, histories, and letters—are readings commonly employed in intermediate Latin classes in secondary schools. While the Institute participants are reading material focused on the theme "From Republic to Empire," they will thus also gain a deeper understanding of authors commonly taught in the schools, of their language, their thought, their lives, and the events that shaped their writing. At the same time, attention will be given to methods appropriate to the teaching of intermediate Latin in the schools.

Similar principles motivate the design of the Latin poetry course (Lat 519P), directed by Professor LaFleur. The principal textbook employed is Jenney, et al., *Fourth Year Latin* (8), one of the most widely used fourth-year texts in the country. Institute participants accordingly gain experience with yet another textbook series for possible adoption in their own classes; and, in the course of the work and discussions in this class, they receive instruction and gain insights into methods and resources appropriate to the teaching of Latin poetry in the schools. Most importantly, however, participants read in the original Latin extensive selections from the poetry of the late Republic and early Augustan Age, in particular the works of the two greatest poets of the period, Vergil and Horace, as well as briefer selections from Catullus and Ovid. The ideals of the Augustan regime were embodied in particular in the works of the poets who surrounded Augustus, and the poetry of the time represents a flowering of intellectual and artistic thought as remarkable as that of the Italian Renaissance. The reaction to the decades of civil strife chronicled in Caesar, Cicero, and their contemporaries led to the lyric outpouring on behalf of the Augustan peace, however it was enforced, that is so prominent in the works of Horace and Vergil. The finest praise ever received in literary form by any governmental regime must surely be the *Roman Odes* of the former and the *Aeneid* of the latter. As participants read selections from these and other works (including Vergil's *Fourth Eclogue* and Horace's *Epistles*, *Satires*, and *Carmen Saeculare*), they will come to understand the thought and concerns of the newly created Roman Empire as they were expressed by the poets of the time, and they can compare and contrast those ideas and principles with the intellectual and historical milieu of the decades that preceded Augustus' rise to power. Again, since the poetry of the Augustan Age is usually that read in Latin poetry courses in secondary schools, the participants in the Institute are studying material they are most likely to be teaching, but in greater depth and with much more of its context intact than is usually possible.

Daily activities in both the prose and verse classes include grammar review, oral-aural exercises, prepared translations and sight readings, and discussion of the authors and texts being examined, all with attention to the rationale and methodology for applications in secondary-school intermediate and advanced Latin classes (Latin III-IV) and, in particular, to the theme of this second Summer Session, "From Republic to Empire." The PLATO program of computer-assisted instruction remains available to all participants for continued drill in grammar and translation, and the University of Delaware software for the Allyn and Bacon and Macmillan textbook series will be available for inspection on the Classics Department's microcomputers (Culley, 5).

3. *"Republic to Empire" Lecture Series*

Visiting faculty will present afternoon lectures on topics centering on the theme "From Republic to Empire," all related to the

Session's required readings in the primary and secondary sources. Professor Robert J. Rowland, Jr., speaks and directs discussion on the roles of Caesar and Cicero in the later years of the Republic; Professor Kenneth J. Reckford lectures and leads discussion on Horace and Augustus; and Professor Michael C. J. Putnam considers the poetry of Vergil and its relationship to the Age of Augustus. Supplementary readings selected in consultation with the visiting lecturers are assigned in advance of their visits; discussion sections led by the lecturers follow their formal presentations. In addition, as in the 1986 Session, each lecturer remains available in the evenings for informal discussion and dinner with interested participants. Hence, participants are brought into intimate contact with major scholars involved in research and publication on the very subjects under consideration in the Institute's second Session.

4. *Paedagogy Sessions and Open Topics Workshops*

The weekly paedagogy sessions continue in the second Summer Session, under the direction of Dr. LaFleur and Ms. McClendon. Discussions focus on methods and materials appropriate to Latin II-IV classes and include presentations by Professor Gerald Culley on computer-assisted instruction in Latin, Professor Gilbert Lawall on texts and materials for Latin II-IV classes, and Professor LaFleur on Latin poetry for beginning students. Ms. McClendon, on Thursday afternoons, will direct optional "open topics" paedagogy workshops in which participants may seek assistance on curriculum, methodology, materials, and any other paedagogical matters.

E. *The Post-Institute Conference*

A Post-Institute Conference will be held December 3-5, 1987, at the Georgia Center for Continuing Education on the University of Georgia campus. Participants will be addressed by the University's President, Dr. Charles Knapp, on the topic of school/college cooperation, and by Professor Edward Phinney, President of the American Classical League, on the future of Latin studies in the United States. Selected participants will read their final essays on the theme "From Republic to Empire"; and all participants will report on their progress and activities in teaching since the close of the 1987 Summer Session (brief written reports on these activities are also required) and provide a final overall evaluation of the Institute program.

III. PROGRAM EVALUATION

Extensive testing throughout the 1986 Summer Session (numerous quizzes and an average of three hour-tests weekly) demonstrated that the participants all obtained a very good to excellent grasp of the material introduced. Regular discussions with participants and detailed weekly evaluation forms indicated overall a high level of satisfaction with the first summer's activities, especially with the classroom instruction and the work of the Institute staff generally. While there were some complaints regarding the exceptionally strenuous academic demands placed on the participants and the length of the work day, participants and faculty closed the Session with a keen sense of having accomplished an academic task that was very difficult and yet at the same time enormously worthwhile in terms of the participants' needs and the Institute's purposes. Evaluation is continuing during 1987 and will conclude, as indicated earlier, with administration of the Georgia Latin Teacher Certification Test to all participants by officials of the Georgia Department of Education during the last week of the 1987 Summer Session, and with a final, overall evaluation of the Institute by the participants themselves during the Post-Institute Conference.

It is the objective of this Institute, an objective recognized and generously supported by the National Endowment for the Humanities, the American Classical League, and the University of Georgia, to assist in alleviating the acute shortage of qualified teachers of Latin in the secondary schools of the United States. The Institute is a major experiment with this sort of program, and it is fervently hoped that it may spawn successors which will in turn produce more and better qualified Latin teachers to fill this clear and pressing need. More immediately, it is the objective of this Institute to provide the finest possible education in Latin and Roman civilization to our 25 participants, intelligent, industrious, and dedicated teachers who can take what they have learned back to their home schools and in turn share the rewards of studying and teaching Latin with students, parents, educators and others in their own communities across America. While the educating of 25 new Latin teachers is only a very partial solution to a much larger problem, it is our hope and belief that this sort of intensive program for teachers can begin the process of remedying the crisis in the teaching of Latin that has become so apparent throughout our country's educational system over the past generation.

For more information on the ACL/UGA/NEH Latin Institute, write
Professor Richard A. LaFleur, Head
Department of Classics
Park Hall
University of Georgia
Athens, GA 30602

REFERENCES

1. Boren, Henry C. *Roman Society.* Lexington, MA: D. C. Heath, 1977.
2. Carcopino, Jerome. *Daily Life in Ancient Rome.* New Haven, CT: Yale Univ. Press, 1940.
3. Colby, John. *Review Latin Grammar.* Wellesley Hills, MA: Independent School Press, 1971.
4. Crawford, Michael. *The Roman Republic.* Cambridge, MA: Harvard Univ. Press, 1978.
5. Culley, Gerald R. "The Delaware Latin Skills Project." *Classical Outlook* 62 (1984-85): 38-42.
6. Goldman, Norma, and Ladislas Szymanski. *English Grammar for Students of Latin.* Ann Arbor, MI: Olivia and Hill Press, 1983.
7. Hammond, Mason, and Anne Amory. *Aeneas to Augustus.* 2nd ed. Cambridge, MA: Harvard Univ. Press, 1967.
8. Jenney, Charles, et al. *Fourth Year Latin.* Rev. ed. Boston, MA: Allyn and Bacon, 1984.
9. LaFleur, Richard A. Rev. of *English Grammar for Students of Latin,* by Norma Goldman and Ladislas Szymanski. *Classical Journal* 79 (1984): 374-76.
10. ———, and James C. Anderson, Jr. "Meeting the Need for Latin Teachers: The American Classical League/University of Georgia NEH Latin Institute." *Classical Outlook* 64 (1986-87): 42-45; an abbreviated, preliminary version of the present report.
11. Lawall, Gilbert, and David Tafe, eds. *Ecce Romani.* 2nd ed. New York, NY: Longman, 1984-87.
12. Morford, Mark, and Robert Lenardon. *Classical Mythology.* 3rd ed. New York, NY: Longman, 1984.
13. Palma, Ronald B. "*Ecce Romani*: A Review of the North American Revision." *Classical Outlook* 62 (1984-85): 42-44.
14. Rowell, H. T. *Rome in the Augustan Age.* Norman, OK: Univ. of Oklahoma Press, 1962.
15. Scanlan, Richard T. "Computer-Assisted Instruction in Latin." *Foreign Language Annals* 13 (1980): 53-55.
16. Syme, Ronald. *The Roman Revolution.* Rev. ed. Oxford, Eng.: Oxford Univ. Press, 1952.
17. Ullman, B. L., et al. *Latin for Americans.* Second and Third Books. New York, NY: Macmillan, 1965.
18. Wheelock, Frederic M. *Latin: An Introductory Course Based on Ancient Authors.* 3rd ed. New York, NY: Barnes and Noble, 1956.

A Model for Latin Teacher Training: The MAT Program at the University of Massachusetts

Elizabeth Keitel

University of Massachusetts at Amherst

The preceding articles in this collection provide ample evidence of the need for more qualified Latin teachers and of some of the difficulties encountered when trying to train them. In this paper, I shall discuss one of the country's firmly established MAT programs, that of the University of Massachusetts at Amherst. After providing a profile of our graduate students, of their previous training and their subsequent careers, I shall describe the format and requirements of the program itself and assess the factors which have contributed to its success, in the hope that this information may help other departments strengthen or implement their own programs in teacher training.

The MAT program was begun at the University of Massachusetts in 1970 by Gilbert Lawall, preceding by one year the establishment of the University's Classics Department. Lawall accurately foresaw the need for qualified Latin teachers and the special role that our University could play in a region dominated by great graduate institutions. He built up the Department around the program, in fact, and one-third of the current faculty have special expertise in Latin paedagogy. All faculty are integrated into the program, either through teaching graduate courses or by helping with the observations of the teaching assistants and practice teachers. Thus far, the MAT has been the only graduate degree offered by the Department, a factor that obviates one recurrent threat to teacher training, competition for resources and students from MA or PhD programs in the same department.

The program generally has from nine to eleven students enrolled per year, each class for the two-year course having four or five members. Criteria for admission, spelled out in a flier mailed to all college Classics departments in the country, and in a more detailed brochure sent to all inquirers, include the following: a BA with sound undergraduate training in Latin (unfortunately, in these days of watered-down Classics majors, not all our applicants offer even this); a minimum cumulative grade point average of

2.75, with a 3.00 average in Classics, and GRE scores of at least 500. These are the *minima*; most entering students are considerably stronger. Students with serious deficiencies in Latin are urged not to apply until they have done remedial course work. Applicants are asked to come for an interview so that the faculty can assess their potential for teaching. We also look closely at the applicant's essay for clarity of expression and for signs of serious commitment to teaching. The essay often reveals that an excellent high-school teacher in the applicant's own past has motivated him or her to pursue a career in teaching. I quote a typical remark from a student who graduated from Amherst Regional High School: "I have my high-school teacher, Miss [Betty Jane] Donley, to thank for my enthusiasm for ancient literature. I hope someday to be able to inspire students the way she inspired me." Generally, the Department can accept only one of every three applicants. We are reluctant to admit more, since we cannot offer them financial aid, in the form of Teaching Assistantships, and this teaching experience is integral to the program.

Here is a profile of our graduate students for the years 1980-85. Since 1980, 32 students have enrolled in the MAT program; 22 have graduated; 8 are currently enrolled; 2 are on leaves of absence. Of these, 21 are women; 11, men. Unfortunately, in keeping with a phenomenon characteristic of our profession generally, we have had very few minority applicants. Only three members of minority groups applied in the past five years; two were admitted. A majority of our students (54%) either grew up in Massachusetts, attended college there, or both. A typical class in these years included one graduate of an Ivy League or eastern woman's college, one graduate of the University of Massachusetts, and two or three students from private colleges or universities outside of New England. The classes of 1985 and 1986 included graduates of Barnard, Pennsylvania, Wheaton, McGill, Cornell, the University of Massachusetts, Trinity College (Hartford), the University of California at Riverside, and Stanford. Schools from which we have had multiple applications in this period include Smith College, Agnes Scott College, Randolph Macon, the College of the Holy Cross, and the University of Massachusetts. Students in these classes presented credentials well above those required for admission by the graduate school. Cumulative averages were around 3.4 or above, and their GRE scores averaged 611 on the Verbal, 552 on the Analytical, and 586 on the Quantitative (on the GRE Verbal scores, the Department's students were significantly higher than the mean for graduate students entering the University). Over 60% of our recent students enrolled in the program directly after graduation from college; another 14% were aged 23 or 24; 14% were aged 25-30; and the last 11% were over 30. Most who returned to school had held jobs unrelated to teaching. One had taught in a private school for three years, and one is a long-time educational activist who was named "Friend of Teaching" for 1984 by the state's teachers union. My personal impression of these students, whom I advise, teach, and observe teaching, is extremely favorable. They are bright, well-motivated, hard-working (all finish the program on time, despite vigorous complaints of overwork), and will prove a credit to our profession.

Employment prospects for our graduates are bright. Most students have several serious job interviews and are able to find the kind of position they want in the area of their choice. The majority of our alumni work in New England or the mid-Atlantic states. Only 2 of the 22 graduates have decided not to pursue a career in teaching. The rest are either teaching in secondary schools, job-hunting, or pursuing further graduate study. Recent alumni are apportioned about evenly between public and private schools.

Let me now describe the program itself. In 1982 the Commonwealth of Massachusetts instituted new, more stringent requirements for teacher certification. Credit hours required in the subject area were doubled from 18 to 36, and three "pre-practica" were instituted. These are short periods of observation, tutoring, or teaching which must be done in a high school before the student can begin his practice teaching. The practice teaching (now called the "practicum") was defined more carefully and more rigorously to include 300 hours at the high school, of which more than half must be spent actually teaching in the major subject. The new regulations also included five standards around which teacher training programs should fashion their curricula: Standard I embraces knowledge of subject matter; Standards II-V require competence in lesson planning, testing, clear and effective communication, and sensitivity and responsiveness to all students.

The definition of the subject-matter requirement for the certificate in Latin and Classical Humanities was drawn up by the Commonwealth in cooperation with Latin teachers and faculty from the University. It requires a knowledge of Latin and an ability to translate; knowledge of the morphology, syntax, and stylistic features of Latin, including reading skills (which we interpret as oral reading skills); knowledge of classical Greek; theories of language acquisition; knowledge of Greek and Roman culture; and knowledge of the relationship between Classical Studies and other fields of knowledge. The wording for this field-of-knowledge standard has been left deliberately rather vague to allow flexibility in individual programs.

Our students are required to take 22 credit hours of courses in the subject matter. They are broken down into one course in Latin prose and one in poetry (a variety of authors offered each year); one course in Latin prose composition; a seminar in the history of Latin literature; advanced Latin grammar; a one-credit course in oral interpretation of Latin; one advanced course in Roman history and one course in Roman archaeology. We interpret the rubric in the field-of-knowledge standard concerning "the relationship of classical antiquity to other fields of knowledge" to include archaeology. Professor Elizabeth Will regularly offers courses in the Ancient City, which focuses on Rome, and the Material World of the Romans, which concentrates on the *realia* of Pompeii. Graduates have found these courses extremely helpful in their own teaching.

The program also requires 16 graduate credits in professional education courses designed to fulfill the four common standards. The Classics Department offers two courses in Latin paedagogy taught by Professors Phinney and Lawall. Each course includes one pre-practicum, the field-based training element, where students present mini-units and the like at the University and at local high schools. (Each student must arrange the third pre-practicum himself. Many return to their old high schools to do it.) The first of the paedagogy courses, Teaching the Latin Language, involves close study of current high-school textbooks and their underlying methodology. In this course, the students also discuss the Cambridge Latin Course, the text series used at the University, and submit their lesson plans for discussion and analysis. The second paedagogy course is Teaching Latin Literature.

As these courses are a special feature of our program, let me describe a semester's work in one of them in more detail. In 1985 Professor Lawall combined the Survey of Latin Literature and the Teaching Latin Literature courses into a single year-long class. Here students each week read selections from Latin authors and secondary scholarship on these authors; they also studied the aims and methods of teaching Latin literature as they have been formulated through the course of this century, and they examined the materials for teaching Latin literature currently available. The "hands-on" activities included the following: 1) a pre-practicum, three days spent observing the teaching of Latin literature at one of the local high schools, on which the student then reported to the class; 2) one group project involving the preparation of Ovid's Daedalus and Icarus story from Unit IV of the Cambridge Latin Course, which the students then taught alone or as a team in a

Latin class at the University; and finally, 3) student preparation of mini-units on Cicero, treating various aspects of his life and writings. For this last project, each student chose one 30-line passage and prepared two lessons on it. These included vocabulary, grammatical and background notes, content and discussion questions, and a comparative passage from either classical Greek or modern literature, with its own content questions. The student also worked up for the use of the teacher a translation of the passage, additional notes on background material, references to secondary sources available for a high-school teacher and suggestions on how to present the material, including a homework assignment for the second class. Suggestions for follow-up projects for the students were also included.

The remaining common standards set by the state are met by courses in educational and adolescent psychology, educational media, and the foundations of education. Students are also strongly urged to take courses in educational testing and a workshop in combatting racism. In the third or fourth semester, the student does his practice teaching for nine credits. Students are also asked to meet several pre-program requirements before or after they enroll. In addition to two years of classical Greek, these include a course in the history of the Latin language and surveys of Greek and Roman history. We also strongly encourage each student who enters the graduate program without a strong minor area (many, in fact, do come to us with such preparation) to do an unofficial, uncertified minor involving at least 18 credits in a modern foreign language or English. This makes the student more marketable, as he can in Massachusetts teach up to 20% of his load in an uncertified subject, and more than half the jobs advertised by the New England Placement Service in 1985 involved Latin and a second language (on which, see Desrosiers, below, pp. 139-44).

The strengths of the University of Massachusetts Latin MAT program in my opinion are threefold. First, it is strongly academic. The degree in effect combines elements of an MA with those of an MEd. Secondly, the curriculum integrates thoroughly the theoretical and the practical. The methodology courses are not the generic sort taught by schools of education but are designed and taught by classicists who are innovators in the field and who address questions relevant to Latin teachers. The two pre-practica built into these courses provide opportunities for students to design, test out, and evaluate their own teaching materials. As a result, students in Professor Lawall's Teaching Latin Literature Seminar, for example, have produced two readers which contain the mini-lessons produced for class and fieldtested in the high schools: *Latin in Its*

Context: Passages for Reading and Discussion, written by members of the classes of 1982 and 1983 and currently available from the American Classical League's Teaching Materials and Resource Center, and *The Romans Speak for Themselves: Selections from Latin Literature for First Year Students,* by members of the classes of 1984 and 1985, available from the *New England Classical Newsletter.* Thus recent graduates of the program already have a publication to their credit and have developed and demonstrated some competence in curriculum design. Moreover, students who teach the Cambridge Latin Course in the University's language classes have been able to contribute new drills and supplementary stories to the revised, North American edition of the text which Professor Edward Phinney is preparing. More experienced teaching assistants are currently trying out the revised version of Unit IV, working closely with Professor Phinney.

A third strength of the program is the amount of teaching experience it provides the students before they take their first job, even before they do their practice teaching. Most students hold teaching assistantships for the full two-years. Each teaching assistant is wholly responsible for two sections of elementary or intermediate Latin each semester, except during his practice teaching when he has only one. Each teaching assistant draws up his own lesson plans, drills, quizzes, tests, and final examination. He has only to conform by covering the required number of lessons each term. Teaching these required language courses is demanding. Sections are large, from 25 to 35 students each, and contain a *farrago* of students with differing abilities, training, and motivation. A good number have learning disabilities and need extra help and constant encouragement. Every teaching assistant is observed three times a semester by a faculty member. The student then has a conference with the observer and provides him or her with a lesson plan for the class observed. The observer marks the student's performance on a sheet which is drawn up in accordance with the five standards prescribed by the state. The student is asked to evaluate his own performance and he is free to see the evaluation sheet and to ask questions.

Two other factors contribute to the program's strength. The Department of Classics has long enjoyed good relations with the University's School of Education. Swamped with undergraduate majors and graduate students, they are happy to leave us on our own. They feel no jealousy for our program, so small and far removed from their main interest, urban education. Instead the School of Education takes pride in our work and holds us up as a model for others. A central certification office, run out of the School of Education, handles all certification applications from the campus, thereby greatly facilitating the process. The director of the certification office, Michael Schwartz, is never too busy to visit individual departments and explain the mechanics of certification to the students. Mr. Schwartz is advised by a board composed of faculty from departments with teacher training programs. This board coordinates efforts in teacher training across the campus, prepares for outside reviews of our programs, addresses issues of common interest, and lobbies the administration for changes in current practices.

Members of the Classics Department have also built up a very effective network to support the MAT program and to provide help and support for high-school teachers in the state. Locally, the Department participates actively in the Pioneer Valley Classical Association, which consists of high-school and college teachers in western Massachusetts: the PVCA offers stimulation, support, and conviviality to local classicists in the form of lectures, tours, and socials. Graduate students are encouraged to attend the meetings and they often meet a compatible teacher with whom they later do their practice teaching. The main activity of the PVCA is an annual Classics Day which draws over 300 students from local high schools. Faculty and graduate students from the University regularly participate as lecturers and judges of the *certamen* and recitation contests. Every other year the graduate students, under Professor Lawall's direction, put on an abridged Latin comedy for Classics Day. The Classics Department is also heavily involved in the Classical Association of Massachusetts and in the Classical Association of New England. Two-thirds of the faculty have served as officers of one or more of these three organizations. Our graduate students are involved in the activities of all three groups, and it is a great pleasure to meet them again later on as alumni at such meetings.

The success and durability of the University of Massachusetts MAT program thus result from the involvement of most of the Department's faculty in the program, the cooperative spirit of the School of Education and the certification office, the support of local high-school teachers, and, of course, the commitment of the University's administrators over the past 15 years. It is unrealistic to think that such a program can succeed if it is dependent on the energy or enthusiasm of only one faculty member or if it is perceived as a threat by other departments in the university.

The University of Massachusetts MAT program, involving a heavy course load and teaching responsibilities over two years (and often a summer), is obviously not suited to the needs of many prospective Latin teachers today. Those currently teaching can often take only one year off, at most, for further training. For them, programs such as Boston University's, which requires only one academic year and one summer, will be the answer. Some teachers must re-tool while on the job. To meet their needs, intensive summer institutes have arisen, such as those at Tufts and Colorado (described below, pp. 71-82, 123-31) or the summer programs funded by the National Endowment for the Humanities at Westminster College and the University of Georgia (above, pp. 31-62). Our profession urgently needs more programs of all three types if it is to meet the need for qualified Latin teachers.

For more information on the University of Massachusetts MAT program in Latin, write

Professor Elizabeth Keitel
Department of Classics
University of Massachusetts
Amherst, MA 01003

The Tufts University/
Classical Association of New England
Workshop and Institute

John W. Zarker

Tufts University

This paper presents a history of the Tufts University New England Classical Workshop, with an eye to the need for Latin teacher preparation programs of every sort to meet the current shortage. The Workshop's curriculum, faculty, successes, and problems are the essence of the history.[1]

The first New England Latin Workshop was offered at Tufts University in cooperation with the Classical Association of New England (CANE) in 1955. Professor Van L. Johnson was the founding father of the program, though for some years prior to 1955 Tufts had offered workshops in such other areas as Religious Education, Criminology, Poetry, and Play-Writing, as well as regular summer courses on such topics as Elementary Greek, Greek Mythology, Greek Drama in English, Classical Elements in English, the Late Roman Republic, and the Augustan Age. With the subsequent addition of Greek Sculpture, Medieval Latin, Greek and Latin Pastoral Poetry, Ancient Biography, and Great Books of Greece and Rome, the summer offerings had become increasingly varied and reflected more sophisticated planning. In a letter dated January 4, 1955, Claude W. Barlow, Secretary of CANE and Professor of Classics at Clark University, wrote the following to Professor Johnson:

> We have voted unanimously to throw the moral support of the Association behind a Latin Institute to be directed by you in connection with the 1955 Summer Session of Tufts College. . . . It is further our opinion that if the first New England Summer Institute is a success, Tufts College

[1] A less complete and rather different form of this paper was presented to the Foreign Language Association of Massachusetts in November, 1980, on the 25th anniversary of the Classical Institute. Especial thanks are given to Professors Van L. Johnson and Peter L. D. Reid for information essential to this history. Tufts Archivist and Professor Emeritus of History, Russell E. Miller, was most helpful in providing additional dates and facts. I have consulted two cartons of original data from the early Workshop years: classicists save everything.

should retain the privilege to continue the Institute on an annual basis. . . .

The first session of the Workshop met five mornings a week, July 5-22, from 9:15 to 11:40. The content of the session was outlined in the 1955 Tufts summer school catalogue and in the Workshop brochure:

> A survey of trends and practices in the teaching of Latin since 1918. Special topics may include: the Classical Investigation; teaching Vergil in Second Year; experimental techniques in First Year Latin; oral Latin; testing and the C.E.E.B. examinations in Latin; vocabulary on etymological lines; visual and aural aids; guidance problems in high school Latin; Latin in the elementary school; review of text-books and accessory material for the classroom or the Latin Club (maps, newspapers, posters, songs, contests, etc.); the use of classical organizations, meetings, and periodicals; and a consideration of ends and means in propagating the classical tradition through Latin, ancient history, archaeology, and allied disciplines. Guest Lecturers. Museum trips. Exhibits.

The orientation of that first Workshop set the tone and content for years to come. The breadth of its vision and its timeliness are evident in 1986; 31 years later, we still are struggling with the content of second-year Latin, experimental techniques in first-year Latin, testing and the College Board examinations, *et alia*. Professor Johnson had sounded the note which continues through his and other directors' Workshops: the combination of Latin language, paedagogy, and Classics through ancient history, archaeology, and allied disciplines. Thirty-one teachers attended that first session; 14 from Massachusetts, 7 from Connecticut, 3 from other New England states, with the remaining from Washington, DC, Wisconsin, Ohio, and Pennsylvania. These students were taught not only by Professor Johnson, but also by John Colby of Phillips Academy, Sterling Dow of Harvard, Austin Lashbrook of Newton High School, plus two other Tufts professors, Daniel W. Marshall of Education, and Natalie Gifford Wyatt of Classics. In addition to extensive bibliographies of articles, books, and textbooks, students examined displays of books, posters, and slides.

The major common activity of the Workshop was a detailed study of vocabulary as outlined by Professor Johnson in his formal report on the session:

> The *problem* was to find out something about the correlation of high school English and Latin vocabularies, a subject

about which we seem to know very little and one which concerns my own belief that Latin in the schools is chiefly valuable as a diglottio study from which the pupil, operating in two languages, gains a new mastery of words, ideas, and the source of accurate expression. . . . In other words, if a child is reading Caesar in the tenth grade, how is this experience related, vocabulary-wise, to his work in English for the same year? Would Cicero, Vergil, or some other author or authors be more useful at this time so far as the vocabulary elements are concerned? . . . The results are interesting, I think, in spite of these many qualifications. The conclusions are tentative, however, and rest entirely upon my own interpretations of the figures: Latin is the most useful foreign language for the understanding of "difficult" words in English: of the 1910 words on Weiner's list, 1460 or 76.4% are derived from Latin. French enjoys rightful prestige for bringing into English 545 or 37.3% of these 1460 words. Other foreign languages are negligible in this connection: Italian introducing only 11 words from the list, and Spanish 2 words.

The total cost of this first session was $109, including $45 for tuition, $7 student fee, $52 room, and three weeks of meals at $12 per week, cafeteria style.

The second year of the Workshop included a continuation of the general session from the first Workshop; however, to permit teachers to return without duplicating their studies, courses were added in the literature, art, and archaeology of the Trojan Cycle and also in Greek Language, introductory and refresher, for Latin teachers. Thirty-four teachers from nine states and the District of Columbia attended the second Workshop, four of them veterans of the 1955 session. The popularity of the sessions and their usefulness has continued to be shown by the number of teachers returning for further work at Tufts. In a letter of January 5, 1956, Professor Barlow confirmed continuing CANE support.[2]

Since then, with the exception of 1957, when Professor Johnson was on sabbatical leave and only regular summer session courses were offered, the Workshop has been held every summer. An Appendix (below, p. 82) lists the sessions, directors, number of courses, and approximate total course enrollments year by year.

[2] Of interest to New Englanders is the fact that Secretary Barlow in the same letter reported 525 active members of CANE in 1956 and that his stationery advertises the 50th Annual Meeting of CANE at St. Paul's School, Concord, NH, April 6-7, 1956. Professor Gilbert Lawall of the University of Massachusetts at Amherst and present Secretary-Treasurer of CANE reported in April, 1986, active membership of 810.

In order to provide variety and depth to the offerings of each July Workshop, and to provide courses for our graduate students and advanced undergraduate majors as well, a number of author and special topics courses have also been regularly scheduled. There is, of course, a built-in tension in such courses jointly enrolled by high-school teachers, graduate students, and undergraduates. The instructor must be most careful to allay the anxieties of the different constituencies. The teachers fear that the traditional students, both graduate and undergraduate, being younger and perhaps more flexible, might "show them up" in class; at the same time, the graduate and undergraduate students are concerned about the teachers' greater maturity and more professional outlook, and especially their greater experience in the language. Yet, these classes with combined enrollments, have in my experience turned out to be equally enjoyable and rewarding for all groups, after initial fears and uncertainties were alleviated.

A number of especially loved and respected teachers have served as faculty of the Workshop, some of them for 10 to 20 years or more. Among the secondary-school teachers on the staff, from both public and independent schools, have been Clara Ashley of Newton (MA) High School, John Colby of Phillips Academy (Andover, MA), Constance Carrier of the New Britain (CT) High School, Dr. Joseph Desmond of Boston Latin School, Austin Lashbrook of Newton High School, Dr. James McCann of Malden (MA) High School, and Arthur Spencer of Reading (MA) High School. Participating college and university professors, in addition to those from Tufts (Professors Johnson, Marshall, Wyatt, Corcoran, Balmuth, Reid, and Zarker) include: Doris and David Bishop of Wheaton College, Claude Barlow of Clark University, Nathan Dane of Bowdoin College, Sterling Dow of Harvard, John Moore of Stanford, Ralph Marcellino, first of Hempstead (NY) High School and then of Brooklyn College, and Vincent Cleary and Edward Phinney of the University of Massachusetts at Amherst. Students have frequently remarked that the Workshop has derived its strength as much from its faculty as from the richness of the curriculum itself.

Since an institution is often the elongated shadow of one person and since the Tufts New England Classical Workshop is, in fact, the result of the vision, energy, and hard work of one person, Van L. Johnson, it would be worthwhile to examine his philosophy of education as expressed in his article, "Latin Is More Than Linguistics," in *Classical Journal* 53 (1958) 290-301. I shall quote two passages still of general interest. After first discussing the value of learning Latin and then commenting on Greek and Roman education, Johnson remarks (p. 294):

> They [American educators and the American public] may discover, as the ancients knew, that man is more than animal—a thinking, speaking, self-directed agent of his own fate, whose judgment, tastes, and character support or wreck what we call civilized existence. *The main purpose of freedom in education will then be clarified perhaps as freedom to be or to become civilized.*

Johnson's statement on the merits of learning Latin is a necessary antidote to the emphasis on reading Latin (p. 298):

> We read Latin to learn it; we do not learn it to read it, or speak it, or write it—unless we are scholars or accomplished amateurs. . . . Latin is a training in exactness, subtlety, discrimination, sensitivity in word and thought—the beginning at least of a process which affects or even formulates the tastes and judgment of a student. He may not read Latin when he has finished his course—in fact he seldom does— but he will bring to all his reading, thinking, and expression certain attitudes and expectations which Latin has induced.

Professor Johnson had thought deeply both about the ends of classical education and about the end product of his Workshop— the student, whether that student be teacher or teenager.

The development of the Tufts New England Classical Workshop has, of necessity, reflected the changing nature of Tufts University and of its Classics Department. Professor Johnson, chairman of Classics from 1952-69, after initiating the Workshop in 1955, became increasingly involved in the planning and administration of the Tufts-in-Italy program in 1950-68 as well as of a PhD program in Classics reinstituted in 1964. As a result of these expanded activities and responsibilities, a series of new directors for the Workshop began in 1961, as seen in the Appendix. The Workshop itself, however, has changed little from the direction or curriculum established by its founder.

Under the direction of Robert E. Wolverton in 1961 and 1962, the Workshop's enrollment grew from 57 to 70 with an offering of five courses (Teaching First-Year Latin, Teaching Second-Year Latin, Teaching Third- and Fourth-Year Latin, The Roman Revolution/Greek Mythology, and Special Studies in Latin Authors). Under the direction of Thomas H. Corcoran in 1963 and 1964, enrollments increased to 97 and 106 with the same basic courses. In 1965 Miriam S. Balmuth expanded the curriculum to include a Latin seminar with special studies in Latin and Greek each half of the regular summer session, and Professor Johnson was scheduled to direct a seminar on Catullus in Italy as part of the Workshop: augmented by an increase in graduate study at Tufts, the 1965 enrollment reached an all-time high of 132. In 1966 nine courses were offered on campus but none in Italy; 118 course enrollments resulted. In the first of Dr. Joseph Desmond's 13 directorships, beginning in 1967, there were enrollments in 11 courses on the Tufts campus plus 2 in Italy. Unfortunately, the Tufts-in-Italy program was subsequently phased out by the University's Trustees because of perceived financial problems.

A portent of the future of the Workshop could be seen in 1966. In response to letters sent to the National Endowment for the Humanities (NEH) by Professors Johnson, Desmond, and Marcellino, a formal proposal was made "to provide fellowships covering maintenance, tuition, and registration fees for secondary school teachers who wish to enroll" in the following course:

> CLASSICS 177. *The Teaching of Classical Subjects in English.* A survey of materials, procedures, and approaches for the establishment of Classical Humanities courses in secondary schools, or for the introduction of more literary, artistic, and archaeological elements into the teaching of Latin.

Although federal support was not forthcoming, despite a convincing proposal, the course, first taught in the 1967 Workshop, continued to be offered by Professor Marcellino through the 1977 session.

J. Peter Stein, who succeeded Van Johnson as chairman of Classics at Tufts in 1969, directed the Workshop himself in 1971; with a return to the older, five-course curriculum, enrollment dropped to 36. Professor Stein was in turn succeeded by Professor Zarker as chairman in 1971. The new chairman has taught in all but two of the summer Workshops since 1972; believing, however, that the Workshop should be directed by talented secondary-school persons whenever possible, he did not himself direct the program but instead reappointed Joseph Desmond to the post, which he held throughout 1972-79.

In 1972, in a major revision of the Workshop curriculum, the longstanding courses in the teaching of first-, second-, third-, and fourth-year Latin were replaced with a course in archaeology, a seminar in the teaching of Latin, a course in Greek, plus Professor Marcellino's course on the Teaching of Classical Subjects in

English. From 1972 until 1983, the curriculum of the Workshop stabilized as follows:

Paedagogy:	Teaching Classical Subjects in English—Marcellino
	Latin and the Return to the Basics—McCann
Greek:	Beginning and Refresher Greek—Desmond
Latin:	Readings in Vergil, Ovid, Medieval Latin—Tufts
	faculty
Translation	
course:	Genre study: satire, epic, or drama—Tufts/visiting
	faculty
Archaeology:	Topography of Rome, Myth, Museums—visiting
	university faculty
History:	Roman history of various periods—offered occasionally

Enrollments between 1972 and 1982 ranged between 32 and 74. Many students returned to take different courses and some complained that the curriculum should be more varied to allow them to return more often. Professors Balmuth and Corcoran returned to direct the Workshop for a year each (1980, 1981).

One course and instructor during this period should be singled out for individual comment. Dr. James McCann of Malden (MA) High School first served in the Workshop as instructor in a jointly taught course, Methods of Teaching Latin, in 1972 and 1973. After a hiatus of two years, McCann developed a teaching methods course titled "Latin and the Return to Basics," an introduction to philology with emphases on the relationship of Latin to the Indo-European languages and on the vocabulary-building elements in Latin. The participants in this course, offered regularly from 1978 through 1986, work independently, preparing classroom-ready vocabulary materials involving Greek and Latin word roots and families.

From 1972 onwards the relationship of the Workshop to the Tufts graduate program, as well as to the undergraduate program (which annually enrolls 1,200-1,400 of the University's 4,200 undergraduates), was questioned within the Department. A variety of academic, administrative, and economic issues were argued, including the perennial "scholarship versus paedagogy" debate, and ultimately a number of changes were made in scheduling, financing, and other aspects of the entire summer school program.

One major problem for the Workshop's participants over the past decade has been spiralling costs. The $45 tuition for Professor Johnson's Workshop in 1955 had grown to $180 by 1971, plus room and board. By 1982, costs had risen, for those teachers who lived in a Tufts dormitory for the four-week Workshop, to $940 for tuition, room, board, and registration fee. In 1986, with tuition at $550, plus a $30 registration fee, $250 room fee, and a 19-meal plan at $68 per week, charges totaled $1,100, excluding books and travel. Financial aid is at a premium, and without it (from a teacher's school district, where partial tuition rebates are often available, or a tuition voucher for assisting Tufts practice teachers) attending the Workshop has become a considerable financial sacrifice for most teachers.

In response to the inspiring leadership of Tufts President Jean Mayer and to the internal academic and administrative pressures alluded to earlier, Professor Peter Reid, upon assuming the directorship of the Workshop in 1982, immediately applied to NEH for a grant to cover student costs of tuition, room, and board for 36 students over the summers of 1983 and 1984. The award was granted and 36 students were selected from over 100 applicants. Six courses were offered, with each student enrolling in two:

Paedagogy:	Latin and the Return to Basics—McCann
	Methods of Teaching Latin—Phinney
Enrichment:	The Trojan War in Greek Tragedy—Zarker
	Mythology and Art—D'Amato
	Athens: The Age of Pericles—Hirsch
Language:	Medieval Latin—Reid

In addition, there were lunch-hour sessions with visiting lecturers, panel discussions led by members of the group, and separate discussion sections. Books and materials of interest to teachers of Latin were on display.

The NEH grant for the New England Classical Institute, as it had been retitled, continued in 1984. There were only 45 completed applications from which the 36 students were selected. The drop in applications was perhaps attributable to competition from other summer, 1984, Classics/Latin Institutes, at which teachers were granted stipends in addition to tuition and living expenses. The 1984 course offerings were identical to those of 1983, except that the Age of Pericles course was replaced by the End of the Classical World, taught by Dr. Bruce MacBain, and the emphasis of the art and archaeology course was shifted to reflect the different focus of the history course. Professor Phinney's methods course involved a practicum in which five junior-high-school students from neighboring communities constituted a class available to the Workshop participants for testing the methods being introduced to them.

Several courses were offered in the regular six-week summer session in both 1983 and 1984 to accommodate those persons not accepted to the Institute as well as our own undergraduates. These courses, enrolling 21 in 1983 and 37 in 1984, allowed Institute participants a broader curriculum and permitted undergraduates to accelerate their programs.

Professor Reid again applied to NEH for a two-year grant to fund a 1985-86 Institute with a central theme of mythology. Each student was to select two of four seminar topics available (Myth in Epic, Myth in Tragedy, Myth in Art, Myth in History), and there were to be additional plenary sessions directed by professors from anthropology, psychology, and religion to broaden the scope of the study of myth.

Although this proposal was not funded, an extension of the 1983-84 grant was provided by NEH for a 1985 Institute. This funding covered the cost of tuition for 25 participants (secondary-school Latin teachers), but not travel, room, board, or books. Three courses were offered, including a methods course jointly taught by Joseph Desmond, Vince Cleary (University of Massachusetts at Amherst), and Linda Ciccariello (Winchester, MA, High School), as well as James McCann's Latin and the Return to Basics and a course in Medieval Latin taught by Professor Reid. Including the two regular summer session courses also offered (Voyage of the Hero and Classical Mythology), there were a total of 67 enrollments in 1985. The 1986 program included James McCann's paedagogy course, and Latin and Greek courses taught by Professors Reid and Zarker, as well as a series of afternoon workshops directed by guest lecturers.

Most recently Professor Reid, with the endorsement of CANE, submitted a proposal to NEH for a 1987 Institute for secondary-school teachers, "Vergil and the Augustan Age," which has been funded by the Endowment. Three seminars on the *Aeneid* are planned, taught by Professors Reid, Schork, and Zarker: teachers with strong Latin backgrounds will be involved in intensive reading of Vergil and other Augustan authors in Latin; those who have some Latin but who need to improve their basic skills will do readings from Vergil and other Augustans, but with an emphasis on language; finally, teachers of English or other subjects who have no Latin training at all will do readings from Augustan literature in translation. The schedules are arranged for the first 14 sessions in all groups to concentrate on Vergil's *Aeneid*, while in the final sessions all groups will read Propertius, Tibullus, Ovid, and Livy. Plenary sessions are scheduled each morning with distinguished lecturers on various topics relating to Vergil and the Augustan Age.

Following the plenary session, the seminars, and lunch, there is to be a concentration on the art and archaeology of the period with visits to a number of local museums. There will be a community of interests among the participants, despite their varying backgrounds, since all will be reading the same materials, hearing the same lectures, and examining the same artifacts. Two follow-up weekend conferences are planned for the fall and spring.

The diverse needs and interests of teachers participating in the Tufts programs can be seen from Professor Reid's remarks in his report to NEH on the 1983 Institute:

> It was clear that each of the fellows had different goals in coming to the Institute. Some were interested in receiving graduate credits. Some wanted a learning experience in fields close to their own discipline. They wanted to try something academic and *new*; it was significant how many expressed a desire to learn beginning Greek. Some wanted to come back to school and be students again, hoping to find new inspiration. And some wanted merely to be a part of the Institute, to enjoy the collegiality and excitement of a month with others in the same profession. Others were specifically looking for new materials and ideas to pass on to their students. A few Latin teachers, who had either recently changed into this subject or who had had no formal training in teaching Latin, were drawn here by the Methods of Teaching Latin course. Two held PhD's in modern languages and wanted to satisfy their curiosity about earlier civilizations.

What do the teacher/participants take with them from the Institute? Professor Reid in his report to NEH on the 1984 program quotes an anonymous evaluation that typifies participant response and might provide a fitting conclusion to this history of the program:

> One of the most positive aspects of the Institute was the feeling imparted by all the faculty, staff, and special speakers, that we as teachers were more than babysitters and performing more than routine functions in the classroom. It fostered a great feeling of self-esteem as a teacher, and reminded me that intellectual growth was still possible, expected of me as a teacher, and available to me. The experience gave me the same sense of excitement at learning new things and refreshing old learning that I hope to impart to my students. Having the (NEH) grant with no "product" expected at the end, e.g., new curriculum, a syllabus, a particular new unit immediately usable in school, sent the message that it is important for teachers to

be learners first and to love learning in order to communicate that same feeling to their students. I had a wonderful four weeks. I was stimulated intellectually, made many new friends, met many colleagues with whom I will retain professional ties, and most of all I will look back with pride at what I accomplished and forward with enthusiasm for putting into practice skills I have learned and using knowledge gained as part of my "repertoire" as I encourage students to be eager learners. Thank you NEH, Tufts, and all the faculty and staff.

It is the participation with, and interaction among, such students and faculty that has made the Tufts New England Workshop and Institute at once a joyous and stimulating personal experience and a most effective means of enhancing the quality of Latin and Classics instruction in the schools.

For more information on the Tufts Workshop, write

Professor John W. Zarker
Department of Classics
Eaton Hall
Tufts University
Medford, MA 02155

APPENDIX

Year	Director	Number of Courses	Course Enrollment (approximate)
1955	Van L. Johnson	1	31
1956	Van L. Johnson	3	34
	(1957: no Workshop—regular summer courses only)		
1958	Van L. Johnson	3	71
1959	Van L. Johnson	5	67
1960	Van L. Johnson	5	59
1961	Robert E. Wolverton	5	57
1962	Robert E. Wolverton	5	70
1963	Thomas H. Corcoran	5	97
1964	Thomas H. Corcoran	6	106
1965	Miriam S. Balmuth	8 & 1 in Italy	132
1966	Miriam S. Balmuth	9	118
1967	Joseph F. Desmond	9 & 2 in Italy	127
1968	Joseph F. Desmond	11	86
1969	Joseph F. Desmond	8	94
1970	Joseph F. Desmond	9	49
1971	J. Peter Stein	5	36
1972	Joseph F. Desmond	5	44
1973	Joseph F. Desmond	6	34
1974	Joseph F. Desmond	5	48
1975	Joseph F. Desmond	6	69
1976	Joseph F. Desmond	6	40
1977	Joseph F. Desmond	6	50
1978	Joseph F. Desmond	4	48
1979	Joseph F. Desmond	4	32
1980	Miriam S. Balmuth	7	74
1981	Thomas H. Corcoran with Joseph H. Desmond	6 & 2 Asia Minor	55
1982	Peter L. D. Reid	6	50
1983	Peter L. D. Reid	6 & 2 summer school	21
		37 students × 2	74
1984	Peter L. D. Reid	6 & 4 summer school	37
		35 students × 2	70
1985	Peter L. D. Reid	3 & 2 summer school	67
1986	Peter L. D. Reid	4 & 2 summer school	49

Learning Latin Intensively:
The Process and the Product

Floyd L. Moreland
Graduate School and University Center
City University of New York

Philip E. Schwartz
Friends Seminary
New York City

In the late 1960s at the University of California at Berkeley, an experiment in an intensive, total immersion approach to Latin was implemented in an attempt to make more meaningful the Latin requirement for PhD candidates in fields such as comparative literature, philosophy, history, and other humanistic disciplines. The experiment aimed to introduce participants to the morphology and syntax of Latin in an unprecedentedly rapid fashion, without sacrificing detail and, in fact, emphasizing detail more greatly than was possible in regular-paced or even accelerated formats. The intent was to move graduate students within a matter of weeks to the point where they could read unaltered ancient texts with appreciation, equipping them at the same time with the technical vocabulary and analytical tools necessary to use standard secondary sources to the fullest possible extent. By including a substantial literary component in a basic Latin program, there was hope of eradicating a widespread view that the Latin requirement was an unnecessary hurdle to be jumped and then forgotten. In recognition of the pressing demands on the time of graduate students, it would be possible for an energetic student to acquire enough Latin to pass the requirement, to have a taste of varying literary styles and genres, and to develop a meaningful, strong tool for research within the span of a single summer. This experiment had a successful outcome and came to be known as the Berkeley Latin Workshop, later to add Greek to its repertoire and to be replicated at the City University of New York (CUNY) as the Latin/Greek Institute.

An unforeseen development was that the program quickly became attractive to undergraduates who, having been exposed to classical literature in translation, desired to read some works in the original language. A number of these ultimately went on to become Classics majors. Indeed, the Latin/Greek Institute at CUNY (co-sponsored by Brooklyn College and the Graduate School and University Center) is now comprised each summer of a mix of graduate students, undergraduates, a few persons who simply want to learn Greek or Latin, and a newly emerging group: the secondary-school teacher who is seeking certification in Latin.

The documented success of Latin programs in the grades in cities like Philadelphia, Los Angeles, and now Brooklyn, the statistical data that indicate that students exposed to Latin tend to score higher on the Scholastic Aptitude Test than those not so exposed,[1] and a general tenor in American education that there is a need for more basic training in linguistic and quantitative skills have resulted in a shortage of Latin teachers in the schools.[2] The shortage poses a real challenge to school districts and administrators: how does one retrain teachers quickly to fill the need, without sacrificing the depth and breadth of preparation which are prerequisites of good, inspired teaching of a subject?

In recent years, the Latin/Greek Institute has had a number of students who have participated specifically to prepare themselves as quickly and efficiently as possible to address this shortage. The Institute has obvious advantages: all grammar, morphology, and syntax are condensed into a five-week presentation, followed by the intensive reading of texts like *Aeneid* IV, the *First Oration against Catiline*, selected poems of Catullus, Horace, and Martial, bits of Caesar, Livy, Tacitus, and others. Work in prose composition is included, and paedagogy used by the team of instructors who teach the course is tight and fine-tuned.[3] All the instructors are experienced college teachers, and each spring all must participate in an extensive series of "presessions" to prepare for the next summer's program. These presessions consist of mock classes, role-playing, critiques of presentations and methodology, timing, fine-tuning grammar lectures and drills, and the development of a clean, concise strategy, which will ultimately make the Institute itself work smoothly. This kind of attention to paedagogy is rarely found in the college classroom outside courses in Education. Students also earn 12 undergraduate credits awarded by Brooklyn College and so find themselves well on their way to being licensed to teach Latin in the schools. Upon completing the 10-week basic

[1] See Masciantonio (6) and LaFleur (4).

[2] See LaFleur and Wilhelm, above; also Lawall (5), Davis (2), Beer (1), and Greene (3).

[3] For a full description of the Latin/Greek Institute, see Moreland (7); also Quinn (9).

program, they are equipped to enroll in senior-level undergraduate reading courses and, in some instances, in Masters-level graduate seminars.

This article focuses on one example of this type of transformation into a Latin teacher—the *magister mutatus*, so to speak—an example which illustrates how the Latin/Greek Institute can fill a pressing need in American education today. In the spring of 1980, the Classics teacher at Friends Seminary, a co-educational independent school under the stewardship of the Society of Friends (the Quakers), resigned suddenly to become a New York City police officer. As a result there was the risk that Latin would be eliminated from the curriculum. On the advice of a school official, an English teacher at Friends Seminary attended the Latin/Greek Institute that summer. Although he had degrees from various universities and 20 years of teaching experience at both the university and secondary levels, that initial summer at the Latin/Greek Institute turned out to be one of his most intense educational experiences. The intensity comes not only from the intellectual demands and the 17-hour days, but also from the influence of the complete dedication of the Institute's staff to Latin and Greek. Alumni of the program view it rather as ex-Marines view "boot camp." While there, it is like a descent into the underworld, but for the rest of one's life, the memory remains vivid and generates considerable satisfaction over a job remarkably well done. The demography of the students who took the beginning program that summer included a high-school freshman, 4 university professors, 3 prospective high-school teachers, 14 undergraduates, and 14 graduate students.

The success of the Latin/Greek Institute is due to the dedication and training of its staff. The best teaching is predicated always on the public rather than private learning of the teachers themselves. Frequently, those teachers who are the most competent are the ones who recognize early in their careers that teaching is the best way to learn. Rather than taking place in the study or the cloister as an individual pursuit, effective education is a collegial experience in which the student and the teacher learn. All the instructors at the Latin/Greek Institute are still students of Latin, recognizing that they may be as effective by being wrong as by being right. If a teacher is threatened by his or her ignorance in front of a class, he or she may be more interested in authority than education. Latin/Greek Institute instructors are delighted by learning and communicate that delight, even at 2:00 a.m.: all the faculty and staff from the directors to the office secretary are available day and night to assist students by phone in the preparation of assignments.

Classes begin at 9:30 a.m. and continue until 4:00 p.m., with only a short time for lunch. Students sit for daily ten-minute quizzes, and after the first week a three-hour examination is given each Monday. For the first five weeks, the students complete on each day one of the 18 units of the text, written by Institute directors Floyd L. Moreland and Rita M. Fleischer, *Latin: An Intensive Course* (8). For example, a typical night's work is Unit 14, which treats clauses of result, substantive clauses of result, relative clauses of characteristic, relative clauses of result, relative clauses of purpose, and indirect reflexives. On the same night that the student has to survive these labyrinthine syntactical structures, there are also 43 vocabulary words to memorize, 49 sentences in the exercise section to translate, of which the student is responsible for at least half, 3 sentences from English to Latin, and 2 passages of extended reading from Petronius and Cicero. Even the most accomplished student—whether university professor, PhD candidate, or high-school senior—rarely spends less than seven hours a night preparing the next day's assignment.

For six of the ten weeks of the program, one attends the Latin/Greek Institute six times a week because there is an optional Sunday review session. Though the schedule says frequently that an activity is "optional," one soon learns that at the Institute nothing really is—optative, yes; optional, no. Once one has prepared the lesson and slept for five hours, one spends a typical day at the Latin/Greek Institute:

> *8:30–9:30 a.m.*: Optional tutorial help with previous night's assignment.
> *9:30–9:40 a.m.*: Daily quiz on homework, which is always corrected and returned by noon.
> *9:40–11:30 a.m.*: Review homework assignment.
> *11:30 a.m.-12:15 p.m.*: Lunch, or a nap.
> *12:15–12:55 p.m.*: Sight translation or Latin composition.
> *1:00–3:00 p.m.*: Introduction of next lesson, supplemented by practice drills in the text.
> *3:10–3:30 p.m.*: Introduction of new vocabulary.
> *3:40–5:00 p.m.*: Optional tutorial help with that day's lesson.

This daily schedule varies slightly during the second five weeks of the program, but the informing spirit of the second "semester," as it were, remains the belief that understanding a text comes from being able to describe the structure of the Latin language, and being able to do that is as exciting an intellectual discipline as literary or textual criticism. In fact, as practically every class at the Latin/Greek Institute stresses, the two processes are closely interrelated. The daily quizzes still demand the accurate description of syntax. Because of the focus on literature, the schedule changes to the extent that major texts are examined during the morning sessions, while surveys, prose composition, and elective texts are treated in the afternoons. The required units and texts in the syllabus are:

CLASSICAL AND MEDIEVAL PROSE: Cicero's *First Oration against Catiline* and selected passages from Einhard's *Life of Charlemagne*.

AUGUSTAN EPIC: Book IV of the *Aeneid*.

SURVEY OF LATIN LITERATURE: Lectures and discussions on the development of Latin prose and poetry from Livius Andronicus through the Silver Age and into the Middle Ages and the Renaissance. Representative passages are translated and analyzed.

LATIN PROSE COMPOSITION: Simple and complicated English sentences are translated into Latin with a threefold purpose—to review basic rules of syntax, to expand basic knowledge of that syntax by applying the rules previously learned to more intricate constructions, and to call attention to matters of word order, style, and prose rhythm in order to create a sensitive response to the art of Latin prose.

CLASSICAL LYRIC POETRY: Selections from the four books of Horace's *Odes* are read and analyzed so that the language and prosody may be understood.

Each student must also study one of the following:

ROMAN HISTORIOGRAPHY: Tacitus

LATE LATIN PROSE: St. Augustine

PASTORAL POETRY: Vergil's *Eclogues*

AUGUSTAN MYTHOLOGICAL EPIC: Ovid's *Metamorphoses*

Advanced programs are also available for those with upper-division or graduate status in Latin or for students who have already been through the basic Institute during an earlier summer. The advanced program, in which six hours of graduate credit may be earned, appeals mainly to high-school Latin teachers and graduate students. In this seven-week program all of the *Aeneid*, all the *Odes* of Horace, or all of the *Metamorphoses* might be studied. During the first week, students review intensively basic morphology and syntax and establish a common terminology. For the remaining six weeks, two major activities are stressed: one activity is translating and analyzing a large body of material. Daily quizzes, special tutorials, and frequent drills are included. Second, in the ambiance of graduate-level seminars, attention is paid to an in-depth treatment of literary and philological problems. Throughout the seven weeks the focus of the course is on aspects of criticism which derive from a linguistic analysis of a text and which cannot be acquired from a translation.

In those anxious days before actually entering the secondary classroom as a Latin teacher, prospective Latin teachers learn at the Latin/Greek Institute not only what syllabus might be taught to Latin students, but even some things about how to teach that curriculum. The Institute's rigorous insistence upon understanding thoroughly the structure of the Latin language suggests that one can devote much more time to studying syntax than was the case even back in the early 1950s when Latin was a prevalent and strong discipline in our nation's high schools. Learning syntax is a geometric skill. Just as in committing axioms to memory, the student learns paradigms and then from these paradigms extrapolates the form and function of each word in a sentence. That a student can generate a perfect synopsis sheet does not mean that an accurate translation will occur. But by the same token, good translation and an in-depth understanding of a text (with its implied subtexts) do not generally occur without a strong grounding in morphology and syntax. It is difficult for students to come to terms psychologically with this differentiation of skills because translation is an algebraic skill: one is trying to discover the value of X, to fit variable symbols into syntactic slots in an elegant fashion. Translation skills develop slowly through experience. That experience, however, is strengthened by the continuous and thorough study of grammar as a goal of learning. Under the influence of the curriculum at the Latin/Greek Institute, three full years are spent studying grammar at the Friends School. Depending upon the competence of the classes, the first two years are spent working through Frederic M. Wheelock's *Latin* (12). Then the second year and a half are spent examining the same material at a more complex and extensive level as it is presented in Moreland and Fleischer's *Latin: An Intensive Course* (8), the basic grammar handbook of the Latin/Greek Institute. Though there is some overlapping in the lexical component of the curriculum, basically the students are responsible for all the lesson vocabulary in both grammar texts and all the translation exercises.

While the syllabus of the Latin/Greek Institute may provide the foundation for a serviceable high-school curriculum, the methodology of the Institute may also be adapted to present that curriculum. The philosophy of the Institute demands a rigorous understanding of language, with heavy emphasis on memory and problem-solving skills. There is no easy way to learn Latin. It involves at every level a substantial investment of time and energy. To pretend that there are 15 or even 100 simple ways or short cuts to the knowledge of an acquired rather than a native tongue is to trivialize not only the subject matter but also education itself. As a result, no selection, no matter how brief, is ever translated without the assumption that the student is able to parse every word. This premise is tested by a daily quiz, which demands a brief and accurate translation but also a substantial knowledge of how the excerpt is structured through the syntax. The first 15 minutes of each period are spent sitting for this tiny examination, which may or may not deal with the previous night's assignment. In fact, it might deal with any part of the syllabus which has been covered. The teacher's interest is in what mastery the student carries about continuously in his or her head, not what can be crammed in the night before an examination.

Are there advantages to a school Latin curriculum which emphasizes language? English teachers retrained to teach Latin frequently find that they teach more English grammar while in the Latin classroom than they ever did when they taught English. In fact, colleagues who teach English value greatly the insights their students who study Latin gain into the nature of language. At the very least these students learn the vocabulary of language study— parts of speech, i.e. forms, and uses of parts of speech, i.e. function: subjects, objects, modifiers, and so on. In addition, an understanding that every word in a sentence has both a form and a function may well be an important foundation for the study of any modern or ancient language. And, in a very fundamental way, this type of training inculcates the development of rigorous analytical precision. Rather than being only a recondite elective, Latin as language study takes its rightful place in the mainstream of education, nurturing those skills and disciplines that society needs most— critical thinking and communication.

It might be argued that, while this type of linguistic training may have its place on the college or graduate level (even here it will find its detractors), it is less appropriate with secondary students where there is greater need to stimulate and retain interest. The argument is predicated on the belief that students at this age need flashier course content to sustain their attention. Quite the contrary has been the case at Friends Seminary, where in 1985 25% of the upper school elected to study Latin, even though Latin may not be used to satisfy the foreign language requirement. Of those students who have studied Latin, 80% go on to take at least one additional year at the university level.

But whatever an individual educator's views might be about the method, content, and goals of his or her particular presentation, the fact remains that the highly structured, streamlined Latin/Greek Institute model provides a productive mechanism for retraining teachers in the schools so that they can begin to address the ever-growing shortage in this area. Many of the instructors at the Institute have as many as 14 years of experience teaching Latin intensively, and the director has been engaged in this activity for 19 years. Participants can glean from these professionals those elements which most effectively suit their own particular needs. At the same time, participants will be acquiring a grasp of the essentials necessary for their new assignments in a dazzlingly rapid and solid fashion while also experiencing a panorama of the cultural and literary achievements of antiquity.

The Classics are being revived at all levels of education in the United States. Many elementary schools nationwide have introduced Latin as an aid to inner-city students who read English below grade level. College registrations have increased in courses in mythology, literature, and archaeology; and language enrollments have risen dramatically at many institutions in recent years. Within the City University of New York, a required course on classical civilization in the new core curriculum at Brooklyn College has been established, and the Latin Cornerstone Project, in which Latin is taught to fifth- and sixth-graders in the public schools on the Philadelphia and Los Angeles models, has generated renewed interest among students, teachers, and parents. The intensive Latin/Greek Institute of Brooklyn College and the CUNY Graduate Center has enjoyed steady growth during the past decade, with up to 120 students enrolled in recent summers. The Educational Testing Service has spent considerable time and money revising its Latin Achievement Test to bring it in line with current methodology in response to the upward swing in language enrollments.[4] Especially dramatic is the situation in the job market. For the 1981-82 employment year, 89 vacancies for teachers of Latin were listed with the Placement Service of the Classical Association of the Atlantic States, about half of them in the Northeast. There were only 47 candidates for jobs registered with

[4] See Ramage (10).

the Service, which means that there were almost two jobs available for each registered candidate.[5]

Perhaps the most dramatic way in which Latin, in particular, has exerted its influence is the documented evidence that it improves one's basic skills in reading and writing English.[6] Extensive studies have involved pretesting equivalent control and test groups of elementary or high-school students with standard linguistic examinations and then retesting the same two groups of students after the test group had studied Latin. The results showed that students studying Latin performed significantly better (their progress was advanced by several months to a year or more) than equivalent groups not given instruction in Latin. Such statistics have played a major role in rekindling interest in the Classics and in accounting for the increased demand for Latin teachers at all levels.

In the late 1960s and early 1970s, it would have been absurd to think in terms of a Latin teacher shortage and the need to offer streamlined, solid training in Latin to teachers to deal with the problem. Then, the Classics profession was struggling to keep its head above water: short of serving the needs of a relatively small number of graduate and undergraduate students in Classics and related fields, intensive programs like the Latin/Greek Institute did not enjoy much prominence. Now, with renewed emphasis on the development of basic skills and with the resurgence of Latin at the primary and secondary levels, highly structured, rigorous intensive programs like those at the City University of New York and the University of California at Berkeley can provide an important resource to train new teachers and to reshape the curriculum in our nation's schools.

For further information on the CUNY Latin/Greek Institute, write

Professor Floyd L. Moreland
CUNY Graduate School and University Center
33 West 42 Street
New York, NY 10036–8099

---

[5] Statistics provided by *CAAS Latin Placement Service Report*, written by Martin D. Snyder of Duquesne University, 1981-82. The statistics are even more impressive in recent years: see further Wilhelm, above.

[6] See Smith (11).

References

1. Beer, Margaret. "College Latin: Classics and Basics." In *Humanities Report* (American Association for the Advancement of the Humanities) 4, iv (1982): 6-7.

2. Davis, Derek S. B. "Revival of Latin Instruction Takes Hold in Schools." In *Humanities Report* 4, iv (1982): 4-8.

3. Greene, Alexis. "Classics Reborn." *Change* 10, xi (1978-79): 20-24.

4. LaFleur, Richard A. "Latin Students Score High on SAT and Achievement Tests." *Classical Journal* 76 (1981): 254.

5. Lawall, Gilbert. "Teacher Training and Teacher Placement: Responsibilities of the Colleges and Universities to the Schools." *Classical World* 72 (1979): 409-15.

6. Masciantonio, Rudolph. "Tangible Benefits of the Study of Latin." *Foreign Language Annals* 10 (1977): 375-82.

7. Moreland, Floyd L. "An Intensive Approach to Greek and Latin." *Classical Outlook* 58 (1980): 5-8.

8. ———, and Rita M. Fleischer. *Latin: An Intensive Course.* Berkeley, CA: Univ. of California Press, 1977.

9. Quinn, Gerald M. "An Intensive, Total Immersion Approach to Greek and Latin." In *Strategies in Teaching Greek and Latin: Two Decades of Experimentation.* Ed. Floyd L. Moreland. Chico, CA: Scholars Press, 1981. 73-88.

10. Ramage, Edwin S. "The Revised College Board Latin Achievement Examination." *Classical World* 73 (1978): 151-56.

11. Smith, Gail. "Latin and Basic Skills on an Urban College Campus." In *Strategies in Teaching Greek and Latin: Two Decades of Experimentation.* Ed. Floyd L. Moreland. Chico, CA: Scholars Press, 1981. 101-13.

12. Wheelock, Frederic M. *Latin: An Introductory Course Based on Ancient Authors.* 3rd ed. New York, NY: Harper and Row, 1963.

The University of Maryland's
Speculum Romanum Project

Gregory A. Staley
University of Maryland

For the past decade the Classics Department at the University of Maryland has been seeking to serve the needs of Latin teachers and students in our region. When a university department reaches out to its colleagues in the secondary schools, the impetus almost always comes from individuals rather than from the institutions themselves. At Maryland, that individual was Robert Boughner, now of Mary Washington College, who in the mid 1970s instituted an annual Latin Day. When I took up his work in 1979, I sought to expand our efforts and, with the support of a grant from the National Endowment for the Humanities (NEH), led a three-year collaborative project in which our faculty worked together with area Latin teachers to strengthen teacher training and to prepare new materials for the Latin classroom. That project has laid the foundation for a Masters program which the Department has just initiated to help train more and better Latin teachers for our schools.

Many of the chapters in this collection have focused on the need to train or retrain teachers in the fundamentals of Latin and of Roman culture at the beginning of their careers. As a result of our work with Latin teachers, I would like to emphasize the need for programs which continue their development as Latinists and teachers throughout their careers. The issue is not just the fact that no undergraduate major, summer institute, or certification program can possibly give teachers everything they need. Our colleagues in the secondary schools need our constant support, and that support must be more than just moral. Latin teachers need concrete help with the daily demands of teaching. Latin is often not their only subject, and Latin classes are frequently combined so that for each class period there may be two preparations. As a result, Latin teachers have too little time to explore new areas of knowledge or to prepare special lesson plans.

When we began to ask ourselves and local teachers how we might better serve their needs, we soon focused on these two problems: the need of most Latin teachers for in-service training and the great need for new and more varied teaching materials.

Initially our Department's efforts at outreach had been focused entirely on Latin Day, an annual program which at first brought 350 students to campus and which ultimately attracted an audience of over 2,500. Beginning in 1979, I sought to give these Latin Days a thematic focus; the anniversary of Pompeii's destruction that year suggested an obvious topic. In subsequent years we focused on the Olympic games, ancient elections and politics, Washington and Rome as two cities to which all roads lead, laughter and entertainment in the Roman world, and the concept of the hero in mythology. Because the material in these programs was not directly connected to what the students were regularly doing in their classrooms, I was concerned that these field trips to campus ran the risk of being escapes from education rather than journeys into it. As a small way of responding to this difficulty, I prepared a mini-lesson on Pliny's letters concerning the eruption of Mt. Vesuvius for our Latin Day on Pompeii in 1979. My goal was to create a mechanism whereby teachers could follow up on what the students had learned during their visit to campus. The lesson contained suggestions for how to teach Pliny's letters (in English, if necessary) and was accompanied by slides that illustrated the places and events which Pliny described. The lesson itself was unsatisfactory in several ways, but the idea of the lesson clearly had promise, based on the appreciative response we received from teachers. We continued to produce lesson plans to accompany each of our Latin Days, and from this effort an idea emerged for how, through a single effort, to meet both of the problems which teachers faced: by a collaborative effort between teachers and faculty we could provide teachers with additional training and at the same time produce more and better lesson materials.

New materials were needed to supplement the traditional textbooks, not just because Latin teachers were overworked, but also because those textbooks often did justice neither to Latin nor to the Romans. In its 1979 report, the President's Commission on Foreign Language and International Studies emphasized that the study of a language should also be the study of people and ideas: "Foreign language instruction at any level should be a humanistic pursuit intended to sensitize students to other cultures, to the relativity of values, to appreciation of similarities among peoples and respect for the differences among them" (Commission, 1, p. 28). Unfortunately, Latin education has not always met this challenge. As Gilbert Lawall has remarked, "Our Latin courses have tended to concentrate on mastery of the language per se and to regard . . . other objectives as peripheral at best" (Lawall, 2, p. 12). Nothing illustrates this point better than the Latin which students are asked to translate in the most commonly used Latin textbooks. Here is a sampling: "Men fight and women watch." "The good girl is calling the sailors together." "On account of the danger, your small son will carry a sword." "Marcus, what do you have under your toga?" and "The teachers did not often look at the boys with great friendliness." Obviously these sentences were created to reinforce particular grammatical principles, but what about the culture which they teach? They tell us little about the Romans, but much, albeit unflattering, about ourselves. It is little wonder that students sometimes consider Latin useless. As Lorraine Strasheim has so aptly noted, "Latin students have become frustrated with the months and months they spend in learning the 'code' while never receiving a message in real Latin" (Strasheim, 4, p. 7).

Because students needed to receive messages in real Latin and because teachers needed support in preparing those messages, we sought in 1980 a grant from NEH to conduct a three-year program in which our faculty worked together with teachers to address these needs. Teams composed of three teachers and one University faculty member collaborated over a period of six months to prepare a mini-lesson which used real Latin as the primary vehicle for introducing students to some aspect of Roman culture. There were five workshop cycles over the three-year grant period, during each of which four to five teams were at work. A total of 64 teachers and 10 University faculty took part in the project. Not every team created a successful lesson, but the lessons were not our most important product. Rather, our primary goal was to boost teachers' morale, to provide them with a model for how to strengthen their knowledge, and to enable our own faculty to profit from what teachers know about the craft of teaching.

When our project was nearing its completion, I selected 10 of the best lessons to revise, edit, and combine in a collection entitled *Speculum Romanum,* "A Roman Mirror." The title I owe to Seneca, who, at the beginning of his *De Clementia,* tells the Emperor Nero that he has written this essay "to serve the purpose of a mirror and to show you to yourself." Our mini-lessons were created with much the same intent: to function as a mirror in which the students could look closely at the Romans and in the process come to see and understand themselves better. One of the basic paedagogical principles behind our work was that teachers need to be constantly making links between the students' own experiences and those of the Romans. To help to accomplish this, the lessons were constructed to show that some aspects of life today, such as health clubs or parts of the marriage ceremony, existed or even originated in the Roman world. Or they were intended to demonstrate that certain attitudes and emotions which students experience today (for example, fear of particular days, dislike for foreigners, or a penchant to drink too much) had parallels among the Romans. *Speculum Romanum* is now available to teachers through the American Classical League's Teaching Materials and Resource Center and is widely used (Staley, 3).

How did the project work as a method of teacher training? Its virtues were not those of a formal course with a tightly structured sequence of activities and the potential for breadth of scope. Rather, our program offered teachers the chance to develop confidence in themselves and to learn from colleagues in other areas of the state; and, most importantly, it showed them how they could continue the process of learning on their own. The confidence came from dealing with a university faculty member on a one-to-one basis, from working as a colleague to produce something that would bear the teacher's name and serve teachers all over the nation. Invariably, teachers who participated in our workshops reported a renewed sense of pride and of mission. By ensuring that each team was comprised of teachers from different school systems and with different levels of experience, we opened lines of communication and developed lasting relationships that helped both the experienced teacher and the novice. And finally, we offered participants a paradigm for continuing the process of teaching themselves. At the beginning of each workshop cycle, teachers told us that they didn't know where to look for Latin texts on a given topic or where to find secondary material on particular cultural issues. They told us that they were unsure whether they could read the Latin to which they would be exposed. Here the college faculty member on each team proved particularly helpful. Often teams would meet in a library, and the professor shared with the teachers his or her experience in tracking down a source or in working through a passage of Latin. Each of our lesson plans included an introduction which put the lesson topic in a broader context, Latin passages, grammatical and background information on the passages, translations, discussion questions, suggested projects, slides, and a bibliography. In preparing each of these elements on a limited topic and with the help of others, participants were able to learn a great deal within a short time and with a reasonable amount of effort.

One of the most valuable consequences of our project has simply been the fact that it has made other forms of interaction with teachers possible. Several teachers have since been taking upper-level Latin courses in our Department, and we have even begun to invite teachers to teach in our Department. During summer 1986 Maureen O'Donnell, the highly successful Latin teacher at W. T. Woodson High School in Fairfax, VA, taught a course for teachers on the paedagogy of Latin I. The success of our efforts with teachers and the needs which those efforts brought to light have been instrumental in our obtaining state approval to offer a new Masters degree, beginning in fall, 1987. Teachers and school administrators are now quick to call on us when they need help of any kind.

Our project has made clear several issues in Latin education today, issues with important implications:

1. In helping teachers, we must do more than guide their initial education and preparation for certification; we must continue to work regularly in our support of their work. Annual or biennial workshops focused on concrete paedagogical needs are extremely valuable.
2. There is a great demand for everyday teaching materials. When faculty and teachers meet, they should regularly aim to produce something on paper which can be shared with other teachers.
3. Those members of our profession who seem to be most successful at forging links between different levels of Latin education are often those who have themselves taught at different levels. It needs to be part of the graduate curriculum in Classics that future professors meet and work with secondary-school teachers and students so that the value of collaboration is emphasized from the very beginning.
4. Faculty work with teachers and students should be recognized and encouraged by colleges and universities. The American Philological Association and the American Classical League could help in this regard by establishing annual awards to honor individuals and programs which have been successful at fostering the study of Latin through school/college collaboration. Individual institutions could give greater weight to the importance of such collaborative efforts in making decisions about tenure and promotion.
5. In order to help teachers, college faculty need a better understanding of the high-school setting. A program of exchange between teachers and college faculty would be a valuable means of strengthening our mutual understanding. The faculty exchange might be for as short a time as one month or for as long as a semester or a full academic year. The secondary-school teacher would bring to the university

an instinct for paedagogy and in return enjoy the opportunity of enrolling in advanced courses. The college faculty member would become more attuned to the world from which his undergraduate students come and at the same time provide other teachers in the host school with a resource for additional training in facets of the ancient world appropriate to the subjects they teach.

At the University of Maryland we have learned that reaching out to work with teachers and students of Latin in the schools requires a significant investment of time, talent, and energy. Anyone who has studied the *Aeneid*, however, realizes that a concern for the past has to be coupled with an energetic cultivation of the future.

For further information on the University of Maryland's school/college collaborative programs, write

Professor Gregory A. Staley
Department of Classics
4220 Jimenez Hall
University of Maryland
College Park, MD 20742

For ordering information on the Speculum Romanum materials, write

American Classical League
Teaching Materials and Resource Center
Miami University
Oxford, OH 45056

REFERENCES

1. Commission on Foreign Language and International Studies. *Strength through Wisdom: A Critique of U.S. Capability.* Washington, DC: USGPO, 1979.

2. Lawall, Gilbert. "Latin: Directions for the 1980s." Unpublished essay presented to the Classical Association of Maine. 1 Oct. 1980.

3. Staley, Gregory A., ed. *Speculum Romanum.* Oxford, OH: ACL Teaching Materials and Resource Center, n.d. (TMRC item B315).

4. Strasheim, Lorraine. "Some Working Hypotheses for Latin Education in American Secondary Schools in the Next Decade." Oxford, OH: ACL Teaching Materials and Resource Center, n.d. (TMRC item B6).

Programs for Latin Teachers at the University of Virginia

Sally Davis
Wakefield High School
Arlington, Virginia

Jon D. Mikalson
University of Virginia

For 75 years high-school teachers and college faculty of the Commonwealth of Virginia have met semiannually and shared in a multitude of joint projects under the aegis of the Classical Association of Virginia. Over the years the leadership of the Association has so carefully respected the mutual and separate concerns of teachers and professors that the interest of both has been sustained. As a result many teachers and faculty in Virginia have come to know one another well, and have come to realize that they are colleagues with shared purposes.

One of the many fruits of this collegiality has been the development, at the University of Virginia, of a program designed to improve the quality and augment the growth of the teaching of Latin in the schools of Virginia. The program has a number of elements, but its cornerstone is Latin 701, the Teaching of Latin I-II, a course offered by Sally Davis each summer since 1982. This course provides to future and current teachers what—apart from a general knowledge of Latin—they most need to know for the day-to-day business of teaching first- and second-year Latin to high-school students.

Sally Davis is an experienced and practicing teacher of Latin at Wakefield High School in Arlington, Virginia. She has a BA in Latin and MA degrees in both Latin and Education. The course she teaches was designed on the principle that successful Latin teachers know best (surely better than most college faculty) the realities, potentialities, and methods of teaching Latin to high-school students. This is obvious to every teacher, but it sometimes takes an hour or two in the classroom to convince a professor. A university can provide the facilities, a library, a bookstore, the sanction (in the form of credit hours), and a suitable physical and intellectual environment for the course, but a master teacher teaching methods to other teachers is the *sine qua non*.

99

Latin 701 is brief (three weeks), intensive (three hours/day), and conveniently scheduled (in late June and early July). Participants are given materials, examples, and practice for explaining grammar before a class; for presenting material on other aspects of the language and on topics of Roman culture, history, and life; for reading Latin aloud; for preparing worksheets, quizzes, reviews, and exams; and for developing extracurricular activities. Participants with teaching experience bring to the course texts, materials, and ideas they have found successful. Sally Davis contributes her own voluminous materials (some published, most dittoed), maps, posters, and "inspirational" matter. Xerox machines are kept humming so that participants take back to their own classrooms hefty notebooks full of tried and tested lesson plans, study and drill materials, quizzes, exams, and other teaching devices for all facets of the Latin language and Roman culture.

One does not learn to teach high-school Latin from graduate reading courses in Latin authors or from education courses in Child Psychology or Teaching Foreign Languages. Many aspects of teaching Latin are, to use modern jargon, subject-specific, and it is these we address in Latin 701. For new teachers it is a crash course on what they need to know before that first class in September. For experienced teachers it is an opportunity to share ideas and materials. All these benefits are important, but so too is the camaraderie which has developed among the participants each year. New teachers are often nervous at the prospect of their first teaching assignment and welcome the practical and moral support of experienced teachers. Veteran Latin teachers, who because of their subject are sometimes professionally isolated in their schools, develop new and often lasting friendships with other Latin teachers. Latin 701, we have found, provides to all its participants access to the energetic and lively community of Latin teachers throughout Virginia.

Teaching also improves if the teacher learns more of the language and is exposed to new texts and authors. Therefore in conjunction with Latin 701 we offer, at a compatible time during the same three weeks, Latin 725, a course taught by faculty from the Department of Classics. Latin 725 is intended to develop sight-reading and translation skills for Latin prose and poetry. Each course may be taken separately, but together they provide, we hope, what teachers most want and need, in a format and at times suitable to them.

The University of Virginia has been enthusiastic in its support of this program. It has recognized, both in terms of title and remuneration, that the master teacher is a professional, and is, like college faculty, a teacher of teachers. Latin 701 has also benefited from the interest and support of Helen Warriner-Burke, Associate Director for Foreign Languages of the State Department of Education, who each year sends out descriptions of the course to every teacher of Latin in the state. It is advertised also by the University and in the newsletters of the Classical Association of Virginia and the Washington Classical Society.

We intend to expand and improve our program for teachers, and plans for this are being developed through the University's Center for the Liberal Arts. The Center is an organization of faculty, teachers, and community members devoted to the improvement of secondary schools. It is concerned to stress the importance of the subject content of courses, to establish working relationships between teachers and Arts and Sciences faculty, and to marshal community support for secondary-school education. A major goal of the Center is to make available to teachers, in ways they want and need, the resources of Virginia's colleges and universities. The Center has now a project on the Classics in secondary schools, and it is testing a number of options, such as offering Latin 701 on satellite campuses in urban centers like Alexandria, Richmond, Roanoke, and Virginia Beach; offering summer courses, weekend workshops, and in-service programs on topics of Roman history, art, literature, and archaeology; and providing internships, stipends, and other educational and financial resources to teachers. A number of these additions to our program will be available as early as the summer of 1987.

The University of Virginia has also recently revived its MAT in Latin. The degree can be attained in one year, with five courses required in Latin and five (including Latin 701) in education courses. We are pleased now to be able to provide substantial fellowship support for well qualified students in this degree program. The need for such MAT programs is obvious. The demand for Latin teachers is as great in Virginia as elsewhere. In recent years there has been only one candidate for each two or three teaching positions available. School principals are often at a loss in searching for Latin teachers, and, through a Placement Service sponsored by the Classical Association of Virginia and administered by the Department of Classics, we attempt to provide to them qualified applicants for their teaching positions.

Our goal, the goal of teachers and University faculty alike, is simple: to provide more and better Latin in the schools. This, we think, can be accomplished only by systematic and long-term cooperation between college faculty and high-school teachers.

For further information on the University of Virginia's programs for Latin teachers, write

Professor Jon D. Mikalson
Department of Classics
New Cabell Hall
University of Virginia
Charlottesville, VA 22903

Taking an AP Summer Course on the Road

Sheila K. Dickison
University of Florida

Historical accident has determined that the universities which teach Latin in the Florida State System are found in the north and center of the state, while the largest concentration of Latin teachers occurs in the more populous middle and south. In the past, teachers have found it difficult to make the long drive to Gainesville even once a week during the summer, although some have wished to take a Latin course for recertification or to add an advanced course to their credentials. The Classics Department of the University of Florida attempted to remedy this problem in the summer of 1986 by offering an intensive two-week Advanced Placement (AP) Latin class in Vergil at two different locations in Florida, Orlando and Miami.[1]

Since state universities often do not know what their budgets will be until the late spring, the Department got a slow start in advertising the course. Nevertheless, 14 teachers and one well prepared high-school student signed up. For the summer of 1987 we anticipate at least 25 teachers for our course on AP Catullus-Horace.

In order to make the course possible, the Dean of the College of Liberal Arts and Sciences gave the Classics Department summer salary for two faculty members and an additional stipend of $500 each to cover expenses of travel and accommodation for the 10–day period. The Department also provided several hundred dollars to the Orlando group for small honoraria to three outside speakers.[2]

A wide variety of considerations prompted the decision to offer a literature course which would have the practical aim of preparing

---

[1] Thanks to the gracious efforts of Dr. Robert McClure, one group, taught by Sheila K. Dickison, was able to enjoy the lovely campus of Trinity Preparatory School in Winter Park; my colleague, Professor Lewis J. Sussman, arranged to use facilities at Florida International University in Miami.

[2] Outside speakers included Linda Gaskin, Head of Foreign Languages at Edward H. White High School, Jacksonville, who has had experience as an AP Reader and also served on the AP Latin Development Committee; Susan Harper, an experienced Latin teacher and MA graduate of the University of Florida, who did a thesis on Vergil; Bob McClure, who has a PhD in Classics and teaches the AP Vergil course at Trinity Preparatory school.

103

teachers to conduct their own AP Latin courses. Teachers in Florida have recently been under increasing pressure to teach AP; several Latin teachers had previously indicated to us that they had offered AP Latin, but not as successfully as they had hoped. Of the two AP syllabuses, the Vergil syllabus seemed the obvious first choice, since that author is at the center of any Latin curriculum.

My own experience with AP has convinced me that the program helps to improve the quality of instruction in Latin at the secondary level and also to provide students with an introduction to a fairly sophisticated understanding of Vergil and Catullus-Horace. After three years as a member of the AP Latin Development Committee, I have recently chaired that committee; I have also been a Reader for the past several years. The expertise I have acquired seemed something I might usefully share with local teachers. Finally there was the consideration that some teachers might never have a chance to teach a course beyond second-year Latin; our course therefore also had to be useful to those who wished simply to read a major Latin author.

The class was scheduled to meet on the 10 school days between July 14 and July 25. Before the first meeting teachers were asked to read the whole of the *Aeneid* in English (the Fitzgerald translation, 8) and to translate lines 1-33 of Book I. In addition to Pharr's *Vergil* text (9), students were required to buy a copy of W. A. Camps (4), *An Introduction to Vergil's Aeneid* (W. S. Anderson, *The Art of the Aeneid*, 1, would have been preferable but is out of print). Teachers also purchased from the Educational Testing Service (ETS) the new *Teacher's Guide to Advanced Placement Courses in Latin* (Cleary, et al., 7), as well as the "Acorn Book" containing the Vergil course syllabus, copies of previous Vergil exams, the complete 1980 exam, and Chief Readers' Reports.[3]

The actual class met for an intensive four hours a day (with an hour lunch break in the middle) and teachers normally earned three credits for their efforts. We first practiced doing a literal translation of the text (in our case Book II of the *Aeneid*) in order to ensure that everyone understood the grammatical structures in the passage. A large portion of the class was spent in an almost word by word discussion of style. As an aid to our analysis of the

---

[3] These materials may be ordered from ETS at the following address: College Board Publication Orders, Box 2815, Princeton, NJ 08541. The Chief Reader's Report on the AP Latin Examination, with a discussion of questions and answers in the free-response section, appears regularly in the *Classical Outlook* (see, most recently, Cleary, 5); the multiple-choice section of the 1980 exam was published in the *Outlook* in 1983 (Cleary, et al., 6).

text, we made frequent reference to the very useful commentaries by Williams (10) and Austin (2, 3). Teachers were also asked to report on articles and discussions recommended in the *Teacher's Guide*.[4] Participants later revealed that this was the most valuable part of the course: some had never been asked to concentrate on stylistic features before; others had not remembered how artful Vergil can be.

After we had read a section of the text, we then examined the AP questions, model answers, and the Chief Reader's analysis of questions on that text. Teachers found it useful to discover not just the kinds of questions the AP exam asks but also what the question is testing and how students can best be prepared to work with the text in order to answer the question. In this phase of the class, articles in the *Teacher's Guide* served as an important point of departure for discussion of aims of the AP class and how these could be achieved.

Another skill which this course tried to improve was that of sight-reading. Traditionally students have found the sight portion of the AP exam very difficult and teachers are sometimes at a loss on how best to prepare students for the task. During the course considerable time was spent in class working on Vergil text which had not been prepared beforehand. This provided an opportunity for discussion of strategies in dealing with an unfamiliar text. The importance of a non-stressful environment for this exercise cannot be overly emphasized. In the end at least some teachers felt a little more confident in their ability to deal with unfamiliar Latin.

Although some faculty might prefer to have read more Latin than our group did (about 500 lines), I myself am a firm believer in the adage that "less is more." As a result of our close attention to a small amount of text (not only on what Vergil said but how he said it) teachers learned a method of approaching Vergil which should serve them in good stead when working on any Latin author.

As a final project teachers were asked to select 30 lines of text we had not read in class and to do a close commentary of their own. These assignments were not due until three weeks after the last day of class. As a model for this project the class read and discussed Anderson's insightful Chapter 8, which analyzes the last 14 lines of the *Aeneid* and illustrates a number of problems faced by translators.

By the end of the two weeks all participants felt they had learned a good deal about Vergil and some were looking forward to

---

[4] For an extensive list of helpful readings, see Cleary, et al. (7), pp. 52-59.

teaching an AP course in the fall. In letters to the Dean of our College, the class members individually expressed their appreciation for the University of Florida's interest in the improvement of secondary education in the state and for our commitment to a fruitful collaboration with the state's Latin teachers.

Suggestions for implementing a similar program:

1. Work closely with the department chair and the Dean of the college, stressing the benefits of such a course to both the university and the secondary teachers. State institutions in particular often welcome an opportunity for outreach to good teachers and students around the state.
2. If you intend to take the show on the road, make sure you are not encroaching on another institution's turf. Local institutions might be invited to cooperate with you in developing summer programs.
3. Advertise as thoroughly as possible through local classical organizations and, if you are planning an AP course, with the regional AP office.
4. Investigate funding opportunities for teachers (local school districts in Florida paid tuition for some of the teachers to attend).
5. Make an effort to help teachers get back into the text and enjoy the Latin for itself.
6. Set up a network of teachers who already teach AP to act as resource persons for those just beginning such a course.

For further information on the University of Florida's programs for teachers, write

Professor Sheila K. Dickison
Department of Classics
ASB-3C
University of Florida
Gainesville, FL 32611

REFERENCES

1. Anderson, William S. *The Art of the Aeneid.* Englewood Cliffs, NJ: Prentice-Hall, 1969.

2. Austin, R. G., ed. *Aeneidos Liber Secundus.* New York, NY: Oxford Univ. Press, 1964.

3. ———, ed. *Aeneidos Liber Quartus.* New York, NY: Oxford Univ. Press, 1955.

4. Camps, W. A. *An Introduction to Vergil's Aeneid*. New York, NY: Oxford Univ. Press, 1969.

5. Cleary, Vincent J. "The Grading of the 1985 Advanced Placement Examination in Latin." *Classical Outlook* 63 (1985-86): 44-53.

6. ———, et al. "The Multiple-Choice Section of the 1980 Advanced Placement Latin Examination." *Classical Outlook* 60 (1983): 112-16.

7. ———, et al. *Teacher's Guide to Advanced Placement Courses in Latin*. Princeton, NJ: The College Board, 1986.

8. Fitzgerald, Robert, trans. *The Aeneid: Virgil*. New York, NY: Random House, 1983.

9. Pharr, Clyde, ed. *Vergil's Aeneid: Books I-VI*. Lexington, MA: Heath, 1964.

10. Williams, R. D., ed. *The Aeneid of Virgil, Books 1-6*. New York, NY: Macmillan, 1972.

Latin Teaching in the Southern States: Current Condition and Future Outlook

Kenneth Kitchell

Louisiana State University

It may seem odd that a Boston Yankee, with strong roots in Chicago, should be prompted to write of the state of Latin in the South. And yet, the eyes of an outsider are often of use, for they often notice things which, through years of familiarity, have become commonplaces to those more closely connected. Thus did Homer send Telemachus to gape at the splendors of Pylos and Sparta, and so too did de Tocqueville have much to teach America. The present author has no such claims to fame, but has now taught in the South for ten years and has been involved for nine of those years with the Classical Association of the Middle West and South (CAMWS) and its Committee for the Promotion of Latin (CPL). An assessment combining the initial viewpoint of an outsider, tempered by time and the experience of an insider, will, I hope, demonstrate first that the South has special problems and needs with respect to the teaching of Latin and Classics, and, secondly, that these special problems and needs ought to be addressed soon in a way that takes into account the unique nature of the region.

There are always superficial differences between teaching in one part of the country and another. Up in the Northeast, of course, it is pronunciation. Everyone in my high-school Latin class near Boston knew well how to pronounce *Gallier est omnis diviser in pahtes tres* (written by Julius "Caesah," naturally). In the Chicago high school where I taught for two years, I was charmed to hear *te exspecto* translated as "I am waiting on you"—grammatically indefensible but amusing to envision. Likewise, *apud Marcum* was not "at Marcus' house," but was "by Marcus." For a friend in New York, the second person plural is regularly "youze," while in Baton Rouge, of course, we know full well that it is "y'all."

But these are all surface matters, curious at first, but soon accommodated and even enjoyed. More to the point is the larger issue of educational outlook in the South and the way it affects the teaching of Latin and our potential for finding future teachers of the language.

The proper word to describe Latin education in the South 10 years ago when I first arrived, I feel, was "uneven." The disparity of quality between most public schools and their private counterparts was often astounding. This may have been due partially to the after-effects of segregation policies, but it is perpetuated today by economic separatism. Thus, in one expensive private school in New Orleans, honor students are required to take five years of Latin and four of Greek. Yet, in a public school near Baton Rouge in 1978-79, the parish (read "county") allotment, per student, was 15¢ a year plus one package of paper for each teacher. No foreign language was offered whatever. Nor was this an isolated example, but rather a lamentably common one, especially in the rural areas.

A great deal has changed in the past 10 years and the reasons for the changes are many. One, of course, is that the entire nation has been caught up in the "Back to Basics" movement. Simply put, people have begun to notice, and express concern, that their children cannot read and write as well as they themselves could in their youth. In 1983, shock at the presidential commission's report, *A Nation at Risk* (National Commission, 26), spawned a flurry of activity at the state level. A recent count shows that virtually all 50 states have, during the past three to four years, appointed commissions to study the problem, most of them hastily founded in 1983 in response to this report, or similar ones, and most bearing prominently the name of the governor who, as a cautious incumbent or a successful challenger, quickly made education a top priority.[1] Follow-up reports on the state of higher education have been no more comforting. In his *To Reclaim a Legacy*, William J. Bennett observed that in 1984-85 a student could obtain a bachelor's degree from 75% of American colleges and universities without ever having taken European history, from 72% of them without American literature or history, and from 86% of them without ever having studied antiquity (Bennett, 1, p. 13). Equally gloomy pictures have been painted by the federal report *Involvement in Learning* (Study Group, 38) and the Southern Regional Education Board's recent *Access to Quality Undergraduate Education* (37). All such reports are seized upon by an avid press and an anxious populace. This last-mentioned report in particular has precipitated further activity in southern states, and the South too is firmly astride that spirited and noble, but historically short-winded horse of educational reform.[2]

---

[1] See National Education Association (NEA, 28), and United States Department of Education (39), where the programs in each state are described. A few states established commissions prior to 1983: Montana (1982), Ohio (1982), Alaska (1980). But the vast majority of such programs were in direct response to *A Nation at Risk*. Cf. also Jaschik (16)

[2] Jaschik (15) reports on the activity of southern governors following the SREB report. On the ups and downs of educational reform see Levine (20).

The cause of Latin is specifically helped by the fact that virtually every recent proposal for curricular reform has called for foreign language instruction as one of the "basics."[3] In addition to this, the members of the CAMWS Committee for the Promotion of Latin have been exceptionally active in many southern states. Because of their efforts, school districts were made increasingly aware of the benefits awaiting Latin students. Thus, when the bandwagon came flashing by, principals and school boards were quite prepared to leap upon it.

On the one hand, then, there is good news to relate. Latin enrollment is up in the South and is continuing to rise, as all available evidence appears to indicate. And we are organizing: states which, five or six short years ago, had no Classics newsletter, state classical association, or state-wide Latin and Classics contests now have all three. Junior Classical League (JCL) membership has risen remarkably. Latin has once more become accepted, a regular part of the normal educational process.

But with the good news, as all students of Greek literature know, comes the bad. As is so amply demonstrated elsewhere in this volume, we simply do not have the teachers to meet the growing need. In preparing this paper, I called CPL workers in Mississippi and Arkansas. Each could name three or four schools which want to offer Latin, but which had no one to do so. I myself am constantly looking for qualified teachers to fill posts in Louisiana.

In some places needs are being met, but in definitely ad hoc ways, and the solutions are as multiple as the problems. In one school no one qualified to teach Latin exists, but someone is taking correspondence courses. At another, a dual-certified teacher gets six sections of inner-city black students enrolled but faces budgetary restrictions on books and has to cancel one section. In a third situation, an MA holder, uncertified, hops between two part-time positions since those schools were just beginning to offer Latin. Her success at one school produced enrollment to open it to a full-time slot, but she is uncertified and cannot stay on in the very job her skills created. She is "unqualified." Other problems are arising

---

[3] The 1983 National Commission on Excellence in Education (26, p. 70) recommended two years for college-bound students. Utah recently tightened college admission standards with a resultant 200% increase in some high schools' foreign language enrollments. See Bennett (1, p. 22). In 1983 South Dakota voted to require two years of high-school foreign language for admission to its public universities, effective 1987 ("Notes," 29). The trustees of the California State University system have instituted a similar requirement to take effect in 1988 ("In Brief," 11).

as older teachers retire and no one is on hand to replace them. Worse still, some programs stagger along with poorly qualified, frustrated, and sometimes even embittered teachers, and year after year Latin gets a black eye and a bad name at those schools.

Where will we find the teachers then? Can we reasonably hope that PhDs in the Classics who do not find employment at the college level will step in to teach at the high-school level? The evidence seems to answer in the negative. Of the 300 Classics PhDs conferred in 1973-76, 74.3%, or 223 of them, found a college job. Of the 25.7% (77 applicants) who remained, only about 25, or less than 10% of the total job force, ended up in a primary or secondary classroom.[4] How many of these, may we suppose, were attracted into classrooms in the southern states, which, as I will show below, have some of the poorest performing students and lowest pay scales in the country?

Nor are our hopes of attracting PhDs likely to improve. As of 1981, 24.6% of all PhDs in Classics had earned their degrees between 1938 and 1959 (Henn, 9, p. 47, Tab. 2.1). This means, then, that the period of approximately 1980-99 is projected to show an ever opening field at the college level for new PhDs as older professors retire, and we can therefore expect even less help in the primary or secondary classroom from this group.

Many look to governmental intervention to help with the problem. The federal government, however, is showing that its actual assistance to Latin will be, at best, minimal. We are not listed as one of the "crucial" languages targeted for immediate and fullest aid. In any case, the strong movement in Washington for a balanced budget paints a gloomy picture for future education spending plans generally. Others look for help at the state level. In some states this may, in fact, occur. New Jersey, for example, has recently instituted an accelerated post-baccalaureate path to certification designed to entice uncertified BA holders into the classroom (Harrison, 8). But this has not yet appeared to be the general case in the South.[5] It is a hard fact we must face, but one which affects vitally our plans for procuring teachers to fill the increasing number of empty Latin classrooms.

[4] The available data show that 7.5% (22 persons) were in a public school system. Another 3.9% (about 12 persons) are classified as "other," which includes those in private schools (Henn, 9, p. 62, Tab. 2.13): I have taken a generous 25% of this number (about 3 people) as private school teachers. The real number is probably lower.

[5] It will be interesting to follow the fate of the recent request of Governor Collins of Kentucky for one billion dollars for higher education ("In Brief," 13). For 1983-84, Kentucky ranked 33rd in the amount of appropriations per capita ("How the States Rank," 10).

Before addressing the solution, let us examine some other aspects of the problem. Why, in fact, are we likely to obtain little direct help for Latin on the state level? The main reason is a product of the overall status of education in the South today. While statistics can be tedious and, if misused, can obfuscate and even mislead rather than illuminate, let us turn to them for the moment. No single chart or ranking tells the complete story, but in this case the mass of evidence is as unanimous as it is overwhelming. The South is defined by the U.S. Census Bureau as being composed of three regions. The South Atlantic region consists of Maryland, Delaware, the District of Columbia, West Virginia, Virginia, North Carolina, South Carolina, Georgia, and Florida. The East-South Central region contains Kentucky, Tennessee, Alabama, and Mississippi, while the West-South consists of Arkansas, Louisiana, Oklahoma, and Texas. For the most part this study is concerned with 14 of these 17 states and does not deal with Delaware, Maryland, or the District of Columbia. Due to their proximity to the nation's capital and its preselected, more highly educated population, these three areas are virtually never found to behave like their southern counterparts.

We turn, then, first to the matter of illiteracy. How well are our schools teaching our children to read? According to recent figures, an average of 1.2% of the population is illiterate in the United States.[6] While these figures have been challenged by some as too low,[7] they are nonetheless useful for ranking purposes. Of our 14 states, only Oklahoma, with 1.1%, is better than the national average. All the others are worse, with the two worst at least twice as bad (Louisiana at 2.8% and Mississippi at 2.4%). In fact, of the 19 states below the national average, 13 are from the South.

The illiteracy rates are no surprise when levels of schooling or scores on standardized tests are studied. For example, in 1980, an average of 33.5% of the population aged 25 or older had completed less than 12 years of schooling. But the range is wide, from a low of 20.2% in Alaska to a high of 46.9% in Kentucky. Of the southern states, only Florida, at 33.3%, ranked better than the national average, and this figure is undoubtedly skewed in part by the large number of elderly Florida residents born and educated in other states. The remaining southern states make a poor showing. Of the

[6] Judge (18, pp. 148-49), based on the 1970 census; see also Bureau of the Census (2, p. 143, no. 234).

[7] In August, 1985, a joint subcommittee studying illiteracy received a report which attacked the census data as too lax and charged that one-third of the adult population (16% of all whites, 44% of blacks, and 56% of Hispanics) are "total, functional, or marginal non-readers" ("Report Shows," 34).

17 states worse than the national average, 13 are southern, with southern states holding down 10 of the 11 worst scores in the land (all above 42%).[8] The most recent figures show Oklahoma, West Virginia, Arkansas, and Virginia with graduation rates above the national average, but of 16 states below it, 10 are from our region and all of them are below 70%.[9] Arranging the data another way to reveal the average years of education completed is equally informative. As of 1970 the average American had completed 12.1 years of education. Of our states, only Florida and Oklahoma match this level and none are higher. In fact, only 14 states are below the national level and 12 of these are southern, including the 10 lowest of all. The averages for these 10 states range from a high of only 10.8 years (Alabama, Georgia, Louisiana) to a low of 9.9 in Kentucky.[10]

As might be expected, this pattern is paralleled in standardized testing results. In a comparison of the performance of 1981-82 students in the Science Assessment Research Project, the southeastern section of the country was not only the lowest overall, but was the only region to score below the national average in science for both age groups tested.[11]

Average SAT and ACT scores, while they must be interpreted cautiously, are also an indicator of the educational situation in the South. Eight of the 28 ACT states are in the South and these states rank 19th through 28th, holding, with New Mexico and North Dakota, all the lowest places. The lowest average score among them is from Mississippi (15.6) and the highest is from Kentucky (17.9), which may be compared with the national high score in Wisconsin of 20.4. Six states in our region are listed among the 22 states in which students take primarily the SAT. Here there is some better news, as Virginia ranks 9th and Florida 12th. The remaining four states, however, rank 17th, 19th, 21st, and 22nd.[12]

Statistics such as these must to some extent be viewed in the context of how little the southern states spend on education. All the states in question, except Florida, fall below the national

[8] Plisko (31, pp. 134-35, Tab. and Chart 4.1); Judge (18, no. 154, 155); Bureau of the Census (3, p. 215); Children's Defense Fund (4, p. 34, Tab. 1).
[9] "School Dropouts" (35). Curiously, the District of Columbia, so high in other areas, is next to last. Louisiana is last, with a graduation rate of only 57.2%. Of 1,000 students in the fifth grade in Louisiana in 1972, only 638 (the national average is 744) would finish school and graduate in 1980 (Louisiana Department of Education, 21, p. 25, Tab. II.1).
[10] Judge (18, p. 147, no. 154); cf. Grant (7, p. 14, Tab. 9).
[11] Plisko (31, p. 56, Tab. 1.22); see the same trend in more areas in Plisko (32, p. 56, Tab. 1.20, and p. 58, Tab. 1.21).
[12] National Center for Education Statistics (NCES, 24, chart A-6).

average on the amount of public school revenue per pupil in average daily attendance, and, in fact, represent seven of the lowest nine states.[13] Of the 14 deep southern states, all are below the national average in teachers' salaries.[14]

For a brief while, advantageous oil prices, coupled with the so-called "sun belt phenomenon," promised a steady and ever-increasing economic basis for the South. But recent trends suggest that the sun belt phenomenon may have seen its best day (Weinstein, 40; Jaschik, 17), and dropping oil prices coupled with a resurgent northern economy offer little hope for many of the southern states. It has been estimated, for example, that Louisiana loses 50 million dollars in revenue for each dollar the price of a barrel of crude oil drops and that this translates into a loss of some 13.5 million for education. So, while certain southern states have recently shown signs of a willingness to spend long overdue funds on education,[15] one may question whether they will be willing or able to do so in the future. Tax increases are in bad repute these days and in the southern states are voted upon by a populace not always firm in its commitment to education.[16]

With all these factors in mind then, we may return to the question of the Latin teacher shortage and how to respond to it in the South. With federal and state funds at a minimum, I do not think that summer institutes within the deep southern states are the perfect solution. They have been tried at various universities and have met with mixed success. In general, there are not enough of the target population—former teachers who want to brush up, those who want dual certification, beginners—living near the few universities that offer Latin. Even the strongest school systems in the states of Alabama, Mississippi, and Arkansas might have at most five to eight Latin programs. And at least half of these teachers will not need or want further training. For the others, travelling to the university to live there for three to four weeks or more is a hardship. The resultant low enrollments, coupled with the often tight finances of the universities involved, make such

[13] NEA (28, p. 44, F-2, and p. 58, H-12); see also NEA (27, p. 34) for 1983-84.

[14] NEA (28, pp. 25-26, C16-19).

[15] When percentage of change in salaries over the last decade is studied, certain states such as Kentucky, Alabama, Arkansas, Oklahoma, South Carolina, Florida, and Georgia, are often above the national average growth rate. See NEA (28, p. 24, C-14; p. 26, C-20). In absolute terms, of course, they still lag behind, especially in overall educational expenditures (p. 55, H-3; p. 57, H-8).

[16] The South Dakota plan mentioned above in n. 3 is now under serious attack ("In Brief," 12); cf. the cautionary tone of articles such as those of Jacobson (14) and Levine (20).

institutes very difficult to sell to administrators. I believe more will come of the sort of national institute now being held at the University of Georgia, but the total number of teachers such a program can produce is limited.

In the South, we must, I fear, wait for the most part for new teachers to filter up the system. But this is even more difficult than it may at first seem. It must be remembered that the teacher shortage is not a problem confined to Latin. There is a growing shortage of teachers in most subjects nationwide.[17] Further, those who choose the profession have tended too often in recent years to be those who score lowest on standardized tests.[18]

Moreover, there are often sizable obstacles facing those who would teach Latin. Even with more students now coming to universities and colleges having taken Latin in high school, very few come with the intention of becoming Latin majors. Almost none come wanting to be Latin teachers. We generally encounter our college Latin students as they attempt to complete a language requirement. Some are intrigued and we can coax them into one more course and then another. Soon they are late juniors and early seniors and we ask them if they have ever considered a major. When asked the inevitable "But what can I do with it?", we proudly exhibit the charts and figures and prove to them that they *can* teach, that there is a true need for Latin teachers. But when they go to the department of education they find out that they need almost a full year more to become certified. This is an economic and psychological burden that few find enticing.[19]

The following example of such a case from my own experience is memorable, and scarcely atypical. This BA in English in 1975 had taken three Latin courses to fulfill her language requirement at Louisiana State. Deeply interested in the language, she later enrolled in non-credit Latin courses until she was eligible to enter the MA program. In 1981 she left to take a job at a local, Catholic high school which had, like so many others, dropped Latin during the "relevant" 1960s and now wanted it back again since it had become . . . so relevant! Under the new teacher, the program

---

[17] In 1966-67 21.4% of all bachelor's degrees were in education and 12.5% in business; in 1981-82 the figures were 10.6% in education and 22.6% in business (Plisko, 32, p. 132, Tab. 2.23). It is projected that by 1988-89 education majors will receive only 8.2% of all bachelor's degrees (Frankel, 6, p. 63, Tab. 15).

[18] See Peng (30, *passim*) and NCES (24, p. 27 and chart A-6) for informative charts and statistics. The latest data show a very slight increase in SAT scores among those who indicate a possible career in education, but their scores are still 70 points below the norm (Evangelauf, 5).

[19] See the examples cited in Harrison (8), and cf. McMahon (22).

flourished for three years. As enrollment grew, an enthusiastic JCL chapter was developed and the teacher's students won many an award. The school demanded only that she take 12 hours of education courses to match those she had taken as an undergraduate. But investigating further, she found that for full certification 30 additional hours were necessary, including 12 hours of practice teaching (still required, although she had been a visibly effective teacher for three years). And—here is the rub—to practice teach, the teacher would have to quit her job, since private school teachers may not act as supervisors, this even though there were no qualified supervisors in Latin in the area. The only ones who had the credentials to supervise were in the gifted and talented program, because they were excellent teachers. Naturally (need it be said?), regulations forbade gifted and talented teachers from supervising. The solution? Have this woman practice teach in English, her minor. She blocked this move by removing English as her minor, forcing their hand. At this time the methods course in which she enrolled was taught by a teacher of Spanish, even though the students in the course included three Latin majors and only one Spanish major and even though a fully certified MAT in the Classics Department had offered to teach the course.

Those who enjoy a happy ending will be pleased to learn that after some four years, the woman finally received her full certificate and did not have to practice teach. But how many have this sort of energy and perseverance? And even if every one did, how soon would they see the classroom? We must find better and more feasible ways to recruit and support the progress of our Latin teachers in the South.

Three avenues suggest themselves. The first is to try again to retrain teachers who are already certified in other fields. If every college or university Classics department cannot support an MAT program or some kind of summer institute (MAT programs have recently been proposed and rejected at institutions in Mississippi and Louisiana), then additional scholarships should be made available to allow those interested to participate in programs out of their locality or even out of state. Existing college or departmental scholarships might be earmarked for teachers studying in the summer, as has recently been approved by the University of Georgia Classics Department; alumni support might be solicited for seeding new scholarship funds for this purpose. Professional organizations should take an even greater role in this area: the CAMWS Teacher Scholarship program is currently being revised and broadened to concentrate on helping teachers become certified in Latin. The same should be done for the ACL McKinlay

Scholarships; and the American Philological Association, as well as local, state, and other regional Classics professional organizations, should establish similar programs. We must ease the financial burden for experienced teachers seeking to add certification in Latin through summer study.

Secondly, someone, somewhere, must hack through the certification jungle. As more states make foreign language a requirement for high-school graduation or for entrance to state institutions,[20] the need for language teachers will continue to balloon.[21] It will be to the benefit of every college classicist to participate actively in his state's foreign language association. In too many states visibility and potential clout are being wasted by lack of cooperation between classicists and their colleagues in the modern languages. With the numbers represented by *all* language teachers in a state, we can work to improve certification requirements and procedures and to advance our mutual interests in other areas as well.

Potentially, of course, university departments of education have a lot to lose: reduce the number of professional education courses required for teacher certification and we cut into education department revenues and jobs.[22] Further, in this time of scrutiny of teachers' qualifications, it is unlikely that the notion of reducing such requirements will be accepted by the public or the legislatures in all states. It could be a form of political suicide right now to appear to be lowering standards, and certain voices are already calling for greater deliberation before major changes are initiated.[23] Still, some refinement of certification requirements is certainly in order and would be beneficial in most states, and this is a process in which classicists again should be involved along with their colleagues in modern languages and in the education departments.

The third avenue of approach is perhaps the most obvious one. Why have we really had a resurgence of Latin? The main reason

[20] Louisiana State University proposes to require a minimum of two years of a language for admission by 1988; some members of the Board of Regents have even indicated that Latin is the language of choice (Redman, 33).

[21] One superintendent of schools in Louisiana was most emphatic: "I'm going to have to put in my classrooms whatever I can find. If she has a pulse and respiration rate and speaks French, I'm going to have to give her a job" (LaPlante, 19, but cf. Semien, 36).

[22] The reaction among the teacher education community in New Jersey was unanimously negative (Harrison, 8).

[23] Levine (20); Jacobson (14). Jaschik (15) reports on a generally strong belief among the nation's governors that teacher certification programs need toughening, not relaxing.

sits holding this volume: hardworking, dedicated high-school and college teachers, who found it difficult, indeed impossible, to accept the fact that Latin was down on its luck and who labored through the 1970s and into the 1980s to effect the renaissance we now enjoy. This is our greatest resource; this is the place we should look to help find teachers for the classroom.

There is at least one thing that every one of us in the profession can do to help: we can begin early to encourage our students to consider teaching as a career. What is crucial is that high-school teachers produce students who come to college, first, with enough Latin to place them directly into advanced courses and, secondly, with a career choice in mind. At the college level we can be sure all our freshmen know early on of the expanding job market. The students, thus made aware, can begin early to take the courses required for certification and will not be caught short in their senior year. This way we can have some good, energetic teachers in our classrooms in as short a time as four years. How soon could we expect this if we waited for the bureaucracies at the state or university levels to grind their mills?

It is a hard chore. The profession is tough and underpaid and currently out of vogue. And the longer those in the South suffer economic difficulties, the worse it will appear. But think. Why are we in the profession? Was there not one teacher who caught us up? One whom we began, consciously or unconsciously, to imitate? One whose zeal made the difference? True, we love our subject, but that love is a contagious thing, and most of us caught it from someone. Mine was a towering, glowering sister of St. Joseph whose picture still adorns my desk. Each of you remembers the figure who played an equivalent role in your development, and it is time to return the favor.

That is your chore and mine. Work with your students early. Tell them that they should consider seriously the prospects of a teaching career. Tell them the joy it can give. Universities and high schools alike can hold career days once a year and invite local teachers and their charges. Seniors can serve as tutors or quizmasters at language festivals and competitions. It will give them an opportunity to taste the profession first hand.

To be sure, it is a tough audience. Materialistic yuppyism is prowling the land, and a life of sacrifice is a hard thing to sell to kids whose cars are better than our own and who feel undressed without a designer name on their blue-jeans. But if each one of us, over the course of our entire careers, convinced just two students to follow in our steps, our numbers would double faster than could be accomplished through any legislation.

We may not be able to change laws easily and we cannot abolish educational bureaucracy. But we can chip away at the problem in the best way we know how, the way we have brought this delightful problem of too many students upon ourselves. We need only combine our hard work and our native enthusiasm to win a few disciples.

For further information, especially regarding assistance available from the CAMWS Committee for the Promotion of Latin, write

Professor Kenneth Kitchell
Department of Foreign Languages and Literature
Prescott Hall 222
Louisiana State University
Baton Rouge, LA 70803-5306

Professor Roy Lindahl
CAMWS Secretary-Treasurer
Department of Classical and Modern Languages
Furman University
Greenville, SC 29613

REFERENCES

1. Bennett, William J. *To Reclaim a Legacy: A Report on the Humanities in Higher Education.* Washington, DC: National Endowment for the Humanities (USGPO), 1984.

2. Bureau of the Census. *Statistical Abstract of the United States, 1981.* Washington, DC: USGPO, 1981.

3. ———. *Statistical Abstract of the United States, 1985.* Washington, DC: USGPO, 1985.

4. Children's Defense Fund (CDF). *Children Out of School.* Washington, DC: CDF, 1974.

5. Evangelauf, Jean. "Efforts to Improve the Teaching Profession Seen Making 'Slow but Steady' Progress." *Chronicle of Higher Education (CHE)* 13 Nov. 1985: 2.

6. Frankel, Martin M., and Debra E. Gerald. *Projections of Education Statistics to 1988-89.* Washington, DC: National Center for Education Statistics (USGPO), 1980.

7. Grant, W. Vance, and Thomas D. Snyder. *Digest of Education Statistics, 1983-84.* Washington, DC: National Center for Education Statistics (USGPO), 1983.

8. Harrison, Charles. "'Provisional Teacher' Plan Expected to Attract New Interest in New Jersey." *CHE* 30 Oct. 1985: 3.

9. Henn, Susan, and Betty D. Maxfield. *Departing the Ivy Halls:*

Changing Employment Situations for Recent Ph.D.s. Washington, DC: National Academy Press (National Research Council), 1983.

10. "How the States Rank on 7 Scales." *CHE* 30 Oct. 1985: 13.

11. "In Brief: The States." *CHE* 27 Nov. 1985: 13.

12. "In Brief: The States." *CHE* 15 Jan. 1986: 18.

13. "In Brief: The States." *CHE* 29 Jan. 1986: 13.

14. Jacobson, Robert L. "Leading Advocates of Reform in Undergraduate Education Find that It's Not So Easy to Move from Rhetoric to Action." *CHE* 9 Oct. 1985: 24.

15. Jaschik, Scott. "Southern States Launch Drives to Improve Colleges' Quality." *CHE* 9 Oct. 1985: 15, 21.

16. ———. "On States' Higher-Education Agendas: Money, Governance, Teacher Training." *CHE* 15 Jan. 1986: 1, 16.

17. ———. "Mississippi Board Recommends Closing 2 Universities and 2 Professional Schools." *CHE* 29 Jan. 1986: 11, 13.

18. Judge, Clark S. *The Book of American Rankings.* New York, NY: Facts on File, 1979.

19. LaPlante, John. "Foreign Language Classes Eyed for Primary Grades." *Morning Advocate* [Baton Rouge, LA] 23 Feb. 1984: 1A, 10A.

20. Levine, Arthur. "Undergraduate Reforms: A Time for Readjustment." *CHE* 6 Nov. 1985: 44.

21. Louisiana Department of Education. *One Hundred Thirty-Fourth Annual Report, Session 1982-83 (Bulletin 1472).* Baton Rouge, LA: Louisiana Department of Education, 1984 (SRI: 84–S8280).

22. McMahon, Bill. "More Qualified Teachers Needed." *Morning Advocate* [Baton Rouge, LA] 7 Dec. 1985: 14A.

23. National Center for Education Statistics. *Bulletin.* July, 1984 (ASI: 84-4838-11).

24. ———. *Indicators of Education Status and Trends.* Washington, DC: United States Department of Education (USGPO), 1985 (ASI: 85-4828-22).

25. ———. "Many College Freshmen Take Remedial Courses." *Bulletin* Sept. 1985 (ASI: 85-4848-18).

26. National Commission on Excellence in Education. *A Nation at Risk.* Washington, DC: USGPO, 1983.

27. National Education Association. *Datasearch. How States Rate: Measures of Educational Excellence.* Washington, DC: USGPO, 1984.

28. ———. *Rankings of the States, 1985.* Washington, DC: USGPO, 1985 (NEA 455 SA/SRI: 85-A7640-7).

29. "Notes on Foreign Languages." *CHE* 27 Nov. 1985: 3.

30. Peng, Samuel S. "Education Attracts Fewer Academically High Achieving Young Women." National Center for Educational Statistics. *Bulletin.* Dec. 1982 (ASI: 83-4838-9).

31. Plisko, Valena White, ed. *The Condition of Education, 1984 Edition: Statistical Report, National Center for Education Statistics.* Washington, DC: USGPO, 1984.

32. ———, and Joyce D. Stern, eds. *The Condition of Education,*

1985 Edition: Statistical Report, National Center for Education Statistics. Washington, DC: USGPO, 1985.

33. Redman, Carl. "LSU Unveils Plan for Tough New Admission Standards." *Morning Advocate* [Baton Rouge, LA] 20 Jan. 1984: 1A, 13A.

34. "Report Shows High Level of U.S. Illiteracy." *Times Higher Education Supplement* 6 Aug. 1985: 8.

35. "School Dropouts—State by State." *U.S.News and World Report* 3 June 1985: 14.

36. Semien, John. "No Action on Tougher Graduation Rules." *Morning Advocate* [Baton Rouge, LA] 26 Jan. 1984: 1A, 9A.

37. Southern Regional Education Board (SREB). *Access to Quality Undergraduate Education: A Report to the SREB by its Commission for Educational Quality.* Atlanta, GA: SREB, 1985.

38. Study Group on the Conditions of Excellence in American Higher Education. *Involvement in Learning: Realizing the Potential of American Higher Education.* Washington, DC: USGPO, 1984.

39. U.S. Department of Education. *The Nation Responds: Recent Efforts to Improve Education.* Washington, DC: USGPO, 1984.

40. Weinstein, Bernard L., and Harold T. Gross. "The Frost Belt's Revenge." *Wall Street Journal* 19 Nov. 1985: 30E.

Meeting the Need for Latin Teachers in Colorado: Summer Programs at the University of Colorado

Joy K. King
University of Colorado

Since its founding in 1877, the University of Colorado (CU) at Boulder has strongly supported the Classics. One sign of that tradition is the fact that our library, named after a CU Hellenist, George Norlin, is graced by an Isocratean-Ciceronian maxim engraved over its entrance, "Who Knows Only His Own Generation Remains Always a Child."

Today the University of Colorado Classics Department remains as dedicated as ever to spreading knowledge of the language and literature of the generations of the classical past. Over 1,100 students a semester enroll not only in our Greek and Latin language courses but also in our literature in translation, mythology, religion, ancient athletics, women in antiquity, ancient history, and art and archaeology courses. Over the years, in order to perpetuate the study of Latin and ancient culture at the secondary level, we have cooperated with the School of Education in training Latin teachers, one or two a year, with appropriate certification, to replace teachers who are retiring or to supply new schools with appropriately prepared instructors.

The result is that for many years, even in the most lean period nationally for Latin in the 1960s and 1970s, Colorado has seemed to many the Oasis of the West, able to maintain strong Latin programs in the Denver-Boulder suburban areas and in Colorado Springs and even retaining programs in mountain towns such as Vail and Grand Junction. In the past five years, just as Latin enrollments have increased nationwide, so, too, Latin has achieved increased popularity in Colorado, as the University's Classics Department has undertaken an aggressive role in offering encouragement and support to the teachers of the state through sponsorship of a Visiting Lecturer program, special mailings for the Archaeological Institute of America and other lectures on classical subjects offered on our campus, the Denver-Boulder Classics Club, and *Colorado Classics*, the state newsletter. This support for teachers will extend in the future to hosting the annual meeting of the Classical Association of the Middle West and South in 1987 and the National Junior Classical League convention in 1988.

At present approximately 40 public high schools and 16 private schools in Colorado offer Latin, and the numbers of students choosing Latin continue to increase as more publicity is given to the role of foreign languages in enhancing verbal competency as indicated by scores on the SAT, ACT, and other standardized exams.[1] Indeed, general awareness of the efficacy of foreign languages as a whole has led the Regents of the University of Colorado to mandate a two-year minimum language requirement for entrance to CU-Boulder. The faculty of the College of Arts and Sciences have followed suit by implementing a long-standing Level-3 entrance requirement.[2] This move has been hailed as a boost for foreign language study. To date, however, additional funding has not been set aside for improvement and expansion of foreign language teaching in the state, nor has there been a resolution of the important question of quality control over the language training high schoolers have received, either through entrance examinations or through a fourth-level graduation requirement for Arts and Sciences majors that would necessitate for most students at least one semester's work at the University.

Thus an increased onus of responsibility has been placed on our high schools, and here, regrettably, our Latin programs are in a weak position. Only 6 of the state's 40 public high schools with Latin have programs in place offering training at Level-3 or higher. These schools obviously are enjoying increased enrollments, thanks to publicity given to the new Arts and Sciences requirement. So are the other languages in schools where Level-3 programs are already in place. Our concern is that unless schools offering Latin institute Level-3 programs, enrollments could deteriorate because of the concern of students that they will not be able to complete the level required for admission to the University. An important challenge in Colorado then is that Latin programs be expanded to offer at least three years of instruction.

Unfortunately, as noted earlier, the mandate for more foreign language instruction in the public high schools has not been accompanied by increased funding for quality programs, so that many school superintendents have not even been looking for appropriately trained personnel to fill their obvious needs. Indeed, as older, experienced Latin teachers have retired, they have been replaced by teachers of English, Spanish, history, or often anyone

[1] On the correlation between the study of foreign languages, Latin in particular, and English verbal skills, see Eddy (2); LaFleur (3, 4); Lehr (7); Masciantonio (8); Sussman (10); and Wiley (12).

[2] For similar moves by colleges and universities around the country, see Barthelmess (1) and other references cited by LaFleur, above, p. 6, n. 12.

who has had any Latin at all and is willing to "brush up."[3] The state accrediting agency has until recently closed its eyes to such violations of certification standards, especially in small schools. During the past two years, however, qualifications have been appraised more stringently, and teachers lacking the necessary training have been required to comply with standards by a specified deadline.

In the face of these circumstances, our responsibility at the University has been seen as threefold: 1) communication with local school districts to let them know that we are aware of the problems and are addressing them, and to encourage them to respond and inform us of their immediate needs; 2) improvement of the quality of teaching at present, i.e., ensuring that teachers are trained appropriately to handle the requirements of Level-3; and 3) increasing the number of available new teachers.

This is the situation then: we perceive a need for more and better teachers and for improved communication with school systems so that they know of our interest in addressing their needs. As for what we have done, and what our plans for the future are, we have felt that, since a very high percentage of our high-school Latin teachers are, in fact, qualified primarily in fields other than Latin (e.g., English or Social Studies), we should attempt to assist them with upgrading their skills through summer session courses, when they can be in residence on campus for intensive training both in the language and its methodology and in related areas of General Classics (e.g., mythology, women in antiquity, ancient history, art and archaeology, and word study). We have instituted, additionally, a special 10-week Accelerated Beginning-Intermediate Latin course (Latin 593-594) similar to the one taught during the academic year for graduate students in other fields who need to acquire a reading knowledge of Latin, but designed especially in the summer term as either a refresher course or as an enticement to teachers accredited in other areas to add Latin to their fields of expertise. It is expected that this course can be offered every other year in the summer session, alternating with another specially planned course, Teaching Methods in Latin, that also meets the requirements for state accreditation.

To enhance the appeal of these courses, the Classics Department has instituted a Master's degree program in Classics with an emphasis on the Teaching of Latin that may be earned through summer-school residency only. The plan includes a requirement

---

[3] Colorado, of course, is not alone in this respect: see Phinney (9), cited by LaFleur, above, p. 8.

of 30 semester-hours of graduate-level courses with a minimum average grade of B (no more than 6 hours of C to be offset by grades of A), four summer sessions of residence or one academic year plus one summer session, and a final oral examination based on course work and a reading list. The courses to be taken include two Teaching of Latin workshops (a total of 6 hours of credit), 9-12 hours of graduate-level Latin, and 9-12 hours of General Classics courses. In addition, a special project is required involving the application of what has been learned to one's own classroom. This project is to be completed and put to practical use in the classroom no later than the semester before completion of the degree.

The summer, 1986, program was the fourth year in which this new curriculum has been in place. Prior to summer, 1983, the program's first year, Classics Department offerings in the two five-week summer sessions included only undergraduate General Classics courses in English plus one or two upper-division offerings in which graduate credit could be obtained, with permission of the instructor, by writing a research paper on an approved topic: summer Latin courses had been viewed as enrolling too few students to be financially viable. The first step in implementing our new plans was to persuade the summer-session Dean to allow us to offer a low-enrollment class (i.e., fewer than 7 students) so long as the average of all our courses exceeded the usual minimum of 15.

We were most fortunate our first year to have Professor Richard LaFleur of the University of Georgia offer the introductory Teaching Methods course and thus launch our program. Neither we nor he knew entirely what to expect that first year, but some of the results are chronicled in detail in his 1985 article in *Classical Journal* (LaFleur, 5). A mixed group of students, including new and experienced high-school teachers, undergraduate majors, and Masters and doctoral candidates interested in the possibility of high-school teaching signed on for the course. Professor LaFleur's aim was to assist teachers and prospective teachers in improving their ability to read and interpret Latin poetry and teach it effectively to all levels of students. In addition to a review of the fundamentals of scansion and the characteristic grammar, word order, and diction of poetry to improve skills in analysis and interpretation, a special benefit from the course was the preparation of classroom-ready teaching units on Latin poetry for first-year students, a project that has led to production of a textbook to be published in 1987 by the Independent School Press (LaFleur, 6)—all in all a model for future methodology workshops. I can also add that one of the participants at this first Colorado Summer Institute was a Colorado Springs-Mitchell High School Spanish teacher, Kendra Ettenhofer, who was teaching, "on the side," first- and second-year Latin. Since 1983, Kendra has built up the program at her school to a full-time Latin position, and one of her students, Lisa Binder, was selected a 1985 National Latin Examination scholarship winner. Recipient, in addition, of a four-year full-tuition scholarship, Lisa is now a Classics major at Harvard.

Since some of our General Classics courses most useful to high-school teachers are lower-division lecture courses not ordinarily double-listed for graduates, we also set up in 1983 what we call an Open Topics course providing graduate credit for certain sections of these lower-division offerings. Graduate students who wish to enroll must attend all lectures and, in addition, arrange with the instructor a special reading list, additional meetings for reports and discussion of the material, and a topic for a research paper. Other classes for graduate students are, of course, provided by traditional double-listed upper-division/graduate-level courses, usually in ancient history and art and archaeology.

In summer, 1984, we offered the 10-week Accelerated Beginning-Intermediate Latin for the first time. A total of 15 students participated, about half of whom were currently teaching Latin but needed a traditional grammar review plus translation and interpretation under professional guidance. Two faculty members shared responsibility for the two five-week sessions. The first session was given over to a formal grammar review—or an intensive introduction, depending upon the experience of the student—using Frederic Wheelock's *Latin* (11) as the text. During the second five weeks, selections from Cicero's First and Second Catilinarians and Catullus' poetry were read. Our impression afterwards was that all participants had benefited from the traditional structured approach used in the course and were prepared to employ more formal methods in their own teaching. All indicated interest in taking more advanced Latin classes from us at a later date. The Colorado accrediting agency allows 16 hours of equivalency towards certification for the 6 hours of University credit earned in this accelerated sequence.[4] Thus two more three-hour Latin courses, taken possibly through independent study during the academic year or by special arrangement during the summer, will allow a teacher already accredited in another field to teach Latin in our

---

[4] The course is equivalent to our Latin 101 (5 hours) -102 (5 hours) -211 (3 hours) -312 (3 hours). Graduate students in areas other than Classics who take the course satisfy our Graduate School's two-year college foreign language requirement.

state, so long as a Teaching Methods course in Latin has also been completed.

In 1985 two five-week summer sessions, each incorporating a selection of courses for students in the Master's degree Teaching of Latin program, were offered. During the first five-week session, the Teaching Methodology course surveyed the history of Latin prose from Cato to Tacitus, concentrating on the development of Latin syntax and the concept of a prose genre. Teaching strategies for the presentation of difficult concepts were discussed, and appropriate materials for classroom use were prepared. In addition, three double-listed (upper-division/graduate) courses were available, an ancient history course (Athens and Greek Democracy) and two art and archaeology courses (Archaeology of Ancient Egypt and Art of Ancient Eqypt). During the second five-week session, the double-listed Roman Republic was taught by guest professor Ernst Badian (Harvard), and the Open Topics special course was Greek Mythology. Thus, a teacher wishing to complete nine hours of work (the maximum allowed for students at CU in summer programs) was able to do so easily.

The 10-week Accelerated Beginning Latin course was offered in the 1986 summer session under the direction of Professors Ernst Fredricksmeyer and George Goebel. The supplementary Classics courses offered at the graduate level included Ancient Athletics (Professor Evjen), Classical Greek Art and Archaeology (Professor Tzavella-Evjen), and Greek Mythology (Professor Martinez). The 1987 program will include during Term A (June 5-July 10) Classical Art and Archaeology (Professor Tzavella-Evjen) and Open Topics: Ancient Athletics (Professor Evjen), and during Term B (July 13-August 14) Latin Teaching Methods (Professor Taylor, Lawrence University), Open Topics: Greek Mythology (Professor Vaio, University of Illinois-Chicago Circle), and Latin Reading (Professor Taylor, Lawrence University). The Department intends, in fact, to offer a varied program of essential courses on a rotating basis every summer; usually at least one outstanding visiting professor will be invited to participate.

So, what are the results of our program to date and the prospects for the future? One obvious benefit to the profession resulting from Professor LaFleur's very successful 1983 summer experiment was that all the participants not at the time already teachers are now either teaching or committed to teaching at some level—a mark of the success of that particular course. We like to think, moreover, that we are offering a "Full-Service" program for teachers—or prospective teachers—at the Masters level, including varied language courses to meet the 21 hours required by the state, as well as related Humanities offerings to provide students with deeper insight into the classical experience and an overview of our classical heritage. We wish that more in-state and out-of-state students and teachers would take advantage in the summer of our pleasant climate and geography, combining professional advancement with the proverbial "Rocky Mountain High." We feel that if only we are able to maintain reasonable enrollments in the teaching workshops and accelerated Latin sequence, the total package we offer can fulfill the essential needs of teachers, especially those accredited in other areas and seeking to add Latin.

Some concerns we do still have include the recruitment of new undergraduate students to the teaching of Latin. As at many schools, our numbers of Latin majors have steadily decreased. On the other hand, we offer a number of large enrollment General Classics courses that frequently inspire undergraduates—often not until their junior year, however—to become Classics majors with an emphasis on Classical Antiquity. One of the requirements for this major, in which we graduate about six students a year, is the completion of two years of Greek or Latin or the equivalent accelerated course. Some of the best of these students take more of the language courses (and only three additional courses are necessary for certification), but, regrettably, fewer each year begin Latin early enough to prepare for teaching certification in a regular four-year program. Certification through the School of Education requires another full year of course work and practice teaching—a total of five years for most students, even if they have planned in advance.[5] In the past, because of the uncertainty of demand, we were conservative about urging more than one or two students a year to pursue the Teaching of Latin program. In this way we have not overloaded our market, and our graduates have always obtained positions. With the clear need for more teachers in recent years, however, we have felt justified in stepping up our efforts at encouraging students early in their undergraduate years to consider teaching Latin as a career. At the same time, we advise that students work toward at least a minor in another field: high schools needing a teacher for a full schedule of Latin courses are still few

[5] For clarification, I should point out that the Classics Department cooperates fully with the School of Education on our campus. The secondary-teaching accreditation courses are wholly under its supervision, but our Department has control over the content of the required Teaching of Latin methods course and participates in the supervision of the practice teaching. Our Master's degree program with emphasis on the Teaching of Latin is wholly independent of the School of Education. Persons needing secondary certification must take additionally the essential professional education courses in the School of Education.

and far between. A student qualified to teach mathematics, history, English, or a modern language in addition to Latin stands an excellent chance of competing successfully for available positions. On this topic, as an addendum, I may note that modern language teachers are now so much in demand in Colorado they can more often teach their subjects full time and are thus less often able to volunteer for "Latin on the side."

We shall continue to work with teachers in Colorado and to encourage teachers from outside the state to join us, both those desiring to add Latin to other fields in which they are accredited and those who need stronger backgrounds in order to expand their programs to include third- and fourth-level courses. At the same time we hope that their best students will continue Latin at the University and contemplate careers themselves in the teaching of Classics, thus fulfilling the injunction gracing our Norlin Library to outgrow intellectual childhood with knowledge of the generations of the classical past.

For further information on the University of Colorado Summer Classics Institute and other programs for teachers, write

Department of Classics
Box 248
University of Colorado
Boulder, CO 80309-0248

REFERENCES

1. Barthelmess, James A. "College and University Foreign Language Entrance Requirements." *Prospects* [newsletter of the ACL's National Committee for Latin and Greek] 2 (1980): 1-4, and 3 (1980): 4-6.

2. Eddy, Peter A. *The Effect of Foreign Language Study in High School on Verbal Ability as Measured by the Scholastic Aptitude Test—Verbal: Final Report.* Washington, DC: Center for Applied Linguistics, 1981.

3. LaFleur, Richard A. "Latin Students Score High on SAT and Achievement Tests." *Classical Journal* 76 (1981): 254.

4. ———. "1981 SAT and Latin Achievement Test Results and Enrollment Data." *Classical Journal* 77 (1982): 343.

5. ———. "Latin Poetry for the Secondary Schools." *Classical Journal* 80 (1985): 151-56.

6. ———. *Latin Poetry for the Beginning Student.* Wellesley Hills, MA: Independent School Press, 1987.

7. Lehr, Fran. "Latin Study: A Promising Practice in English

Vocabulary Instruction?" *Journal of Reading* 22 (1979): 76-79; rpt. in *Classical Outlook* 57 (1980): 87-88.

8. Masciantonio, Rudolph. "Tangible Benefits of the Study of Latin." *Foreign Language Annals* 10 (1977): 375-82.

9. Phinney, Edward. "The Critical Shortage of Qualified Latin Teachers." *Prospects* 4 (1981): 1-2; rpt. in *Classical Outlook* 59 (1981): 10-11.

10. Sussman, Lewis A. "The Decline of Basic Skills: A Suggestion So Old That It's New." *Classical Journal* 73 (1978): 346-52.

11. Wheelock, Frederic M. *Latin: An Introductory Course Based on Ancient Authors*. 3rd ed. New York, NY: Barnes and Noble, 1956.

12. Wiley, Patricia D. "High School Foreign Language Study and College Academic Performance." *Classical Outlook* 62 (1984-85): 33-36.

Challenge, Response, and Continuing Problems: Texas Classics and the High-School Teacher

Karl Galinsky
University of Texas

One of the strongest aspects of the American system of higher education, no matter how vocal the recurrently fashionable prophecies of crisis may be, is its diversity. The same diversity characterizes the interaction of university departments of Classics and the constituency of Latin teachers in secondary schools. No doubt, some general patterns emerge and can be used as a basis for observing national or regional trends. Ultimately, however, the evidence on which such generalizations are based comes from varied case histories. This brief overview of the situation in Texas, therefore, is not meant to provide a universally applicable paradigm; there are the usual local idiosyncrasies which often shape the interaction more than any other factor and, at the same time, provide the necessary human element on which the success of the relevant programs is ultimately based.

In terms of historical perspective, the tradition of outreach programs has been an established one for the Department of Classics at the University of Texas (UT) in Austin for several decades. It is observable already in the 1920s and 1930s, and personal factors and inclination seem to be the strongest determinant. Why do some university departments have stronger links with high-school teachers than do others? The answer often is quite simple: because some of the ranking members of the departmental professoriate care. At UT Austin, the late Harry Leon taught and worked with high-school teachers for many years; when other faculty joined the Department, the tradition simply was there and maintained as a basic component of the Department's mission without any further philosophical debate. Being responsive to the concerns of high-school teachers and collaborating with them became an accepted way of doing things.

Due to the strength and number of the state's Latin secondary programs, the Texas Education Agency established in the 1960s the position of a coordinator in that area. The Latin programs, therefore, received special and individual attention. Again, the individual who was chosen for the position made the crucial difference. Bobby LaBouve, who received his MA in Latin from the University, worked incessantly with teachers around the state, promoted "networking," saw to it that in-service programs were truly effective, and furthered the relations between the University's Classics Department and the secondary teachers. Few state education establishments are fortunate enough to have such a budgeted position; it is definitely worth fighting for.

With this additional impetus, the outreach function of the Department increased. After Professor Leon's death, several faculty members, in addition to their other duties, would regularly serve as speakers even at faraway high schools, supervise Junior Classical League contests, and conduct in-service activities. Openness and accessibility of individual faculty members made all the difference, plus the recognition that such activities did not foreclose the desirability of high academic attainment in other areas, such as scholarly publication. In other words, while there will be always one or two faculty members who particularly work with the high-school crowd, their efforts should not be confined to that area alone, nor should other members of a department be exempt from this kind of service entirely. Wider participation definitely has its benefits. In that regard, the healthy participation of many faculty members in the activities of the Texas Classical Association, which of course comprises mostly school teachers, is particulary laudable.

The interaction goes beyond socializing and public relations (such as teachers from various cities bringing their students to the UT campus on a given day under the aegis of the Department—students always like to change locales). At the heart of our mutual concern is the professional development of the teachers, and we have pursued various strategies to aid them. Their vicissitudes may prove instructive.

For five or six years, from the late 1960s to the mid-1970s, the Department offered a summer MA program for Latin teachers. It conformed to the rules of the University's graduate school in terms of number of courses (10) plus thesis or MA report. Typically, this could be accomplished in three summers' time. The initial clientele was enthusiastic—somewhat less so, actually, about having to take the Graduate Record Examination—but not in infinite supply. The constraints became noticeable on both sides: few teachers were in the position to spend an entire summer away from home, nor could the Department support a number of courses with smallish enrollments that were restricted to a special clientele.

The subsequent stage, therefore, consisted of two summer short courses (two to three weeks) which met several hours a day and, because they were courses in classical civilization rather than

Latin, were open to high-school and junior-college teachers in various disciplines. Some MA's were produced under these circumstances, usually with a few additional individual instruction courses in Latin. Furthermore, departmental faculty started teaching some "outpatient" courses during the regular academic year especially for teachers who had been conscripted by their schools into the teaching of Latin without the requisite certification. Some of these courses, especially in composition, can be handled almost entirely by correspondence; others require at least one bi-weekly conference.

This is still the pattern at the moment. The summer short courses, which included one on the preparation of Latin Advanced Placement high-school courses, are not offered regularly every summer. Individual instruction courses, which can be structured flexibly without sacrificing rigor, are taught during the entire academic year especially for teachers who live in commuting distance from Austin. The pressure on the UT Department of Classics as the sole provider of help to Latin teachers has been alleviated by the creation of an MA Program in Classical Humanities at Texas Tech University in Lubbock (the Austin Department strongly supported its inception several years ago) and by the increasing presence of Classics faculties at universities in the other metropolitan areas, i.e., especially Dallas/Fort Worth, Houston, and San Antonio. All roads, therefore, do not have to lead to Austin; teacher certification programs in Latin are available through various institutions around the state.

A related factor has been the development of changing departmental priorities. With its populist heritage, UT Austin has always placed incomparably stronger emphasis on undergraduate teaching than even the major and first-rate state universities to which it readily compares itself, e.g., Berkeley and Michigan. Especially in the last two decades, a concerted effort has been made—and Classics is a good example—to develop strong research and graduate programs. Furthermore, the Department is quite unique in the extent to which it has bucked the endemic tendency of academe to compartmentalize disciplines. Instead, it is an interdisciplinary area studies program which incorporates all relevant fields and subfields of classical antiquity. The quantitative result has been that it has become the largest Classics Department in the United States, but the qualitative results are even more gratifying: the PhD program is now ranked among the best in the country, and two departmental research units, one in classical archaeology and the other in Aegean epigraphy, are producing outstanding and innovative results. Nor has undergraduate teaching been de-emphasized: the Department teaches almost 7,000 students per year and its student/teaching staff ratio is second to only one other department in Arts and Sciences.

Have the needs of the high-school teachers received less attention in the process? I doubt it. While we have referred several teachers to resources closer to home, which makes excellent sense in view of the size of the state of Texas anyway, the Department operates a busy Placement Service for teachers and schools throughout the state (and even some neighboring states). It hosts an annual conference on the training and placement of Latin teachers and has closely worked with the relevant governmental agencies in the area of the revision of certification standards. Despite having special undergraduate scholarship money for students who are working toward certification, the Department is rarely producing more than two Latin teachers a year, which, of course, is totally inadequate in a state where demand is drastically outpacing supply.

This situation, in Texas as elsewhere, is not the result of an academic de-emphasis on the training of Latin teachers but of the economics of the marketplace. While beginning salaries have been raised for teachers—and Latin teachers can command very competitive salaries—most of our majors are not attracted to the teaching profession because of the lack of economic incentives five or ten years down the road. Typically, our undergraduate majors are pre-med, pre-law, pre-MBA, etc. For a while, the shortfall of Latin teachers in Texas was alleviated by in-migration from the frostbelt—at one point, almost half of the applicants listed in our Placement Service were from out of state—but, as everyone knows by now, even the Texas economy can have its downturn and Texas has ceased, at least for now, to be the golden Mecca in the oil patch.

What lies ahead? Not despair, but more challenges. Given the persistence of schools to find Latin teachers no matter what, there will be more conversions of current teachers certified in other fields into Latin teachers, which means more arrangements—such as the NEH-funded Institute at the University of Georgia—for retraining them and bringing them up to certification standards. Other formats will include more weekend workshops and intensive two-day short courses; the Texas legislature has mandated a system of continuing certification requirements which can be fulfilled in various ways, such as continuing education contact hours, instead of conventional academic courses. In conformance with the return to rigor—the much publicized "No Pass, No Play" rule is a stellar example—the demand for Latin in the secondary schools, including many junior-high schools, continues unabated and is increasing yet more. The ultimate solution is the provision of better than adequate pay for competent teachers at all levels.

I am often told that it is a nice problem to be in a Department which closes most of its courses before the end of registration because of overenrollment and which knows of more jobs for Latin teachers than there are individuals to fill them. I consider the second problem to be more significant because it is a real problem. Departmental resources and commitments are stretched too thin to allow, e.g., for the establishment of an MAT program in Latin; I am not sure it would make much of a difference. While, as can be seen, there has been a great deal of evolution in terms of implementation and strategy, the constant has been the Department's active interest in and concern for the welfare of the Latin programs and teachers in this state. For that reason, it was gratifying to see the first NEH Summer Seminar in Classics for secondary teachers in 1983 being held at the University of Texas at Austin (see Kenneth Pierce, "Summer with Homer and Vergil," *Time* 15 Aug. 1983, p. 39). More recently, the Classics Department has taken the lead in strengthening the relationship between the University and the Austin Independent School District through an NEH Collaborative Projects grant for 1987-88 in the area of world literature. While mechanisms and circumstances change, the underlying commitment of the Department to supporting the schools, especially in view of the increasingly critical teacher shortage, will certainly hold firm in the years to come.

For further information and assistance, write

Professor Karl Galinsky
Department of Classics
Waggener 123
University of Texas
Austin, TX 78712

Mr. Bobby LaBouve
Texas Education Agency
Division of Curriculum Development
Austin, TX 78701

The New England Latin Placement Service: Preserving Latin in the High-School Curriculum

Richard V. Desrosiers
University of New Hampshire

As is clear from the opening essays in this volume, the study of Latin in this country has, over the past generation, both enjoyed halcyon days and suffered damaging challenges. And yet even through the period of the 1960s and the early 1970s, when interest and enrollments in the language declined most rapidly, the Classics profession did succeed in ensuring the survival of Latin in the schools. What helped incalculably to win this victory and to insure its prolonged effect was the hearty and intimate cooperation which has existed between high-school Latin teachers and classicists on so many college campuses. I think it can be fairly said that during the last three decades no other discipline has been able to boast of closer ties and greater cooperation between its secondary-school teachers and university professors. Even so distinguished a scholar as the late Professor Berthold Ullman of the University of North Carolina, whose reputation in classical paleography was no less recognized in Europe than here, never found it demeaning or a waste of time to drive long distances to rural high schools in order to address Latin classes or encourage embattled teachers.

Certainly this sort of collegiality has characterized the work of the profession in New England: a fine example is provided by the conduct of the Classical Association of New England (CANE). Since its inception, the Association's conventions had been devoted primarily to the scholarly interests of the Classics faculties of colleges and private academies, but in the mid-1960s it turned its attention in large part to repelling the assault on high-school Latin programs. High-school teachers were encouraged to become members of CANE, and larger sections of its annual programs were devoted to their practical and paedagogical concerns. In 1975 CANE voted to open its executive committee to permanent representation from the classical associations of the six New England states, which had been working since the late 1960s to coordinate the efforts of classicists in colleges and high schools, and friends of the Classics in the community, to keep Latin from going down before the ravages of the innovationism and parsimony of hostile administrators.

It cannot be overemphasized that Latin programs had never really shared in the extravagant governmental largess which in the wake of sputnik in the late 1950s and early 1960s was lavished on high-school programs in the physical sciences and the modern languages. Since Latin had been forced to survive by its own merits and the dedication of its teachers, it proved stronger, better able to thrive, especially after the mid-1970s, in the wake of the energy crisis and the renewed trend of conservatism forced by increasing budgetary restraints upon secondary-school education.

The experience in New England was, I believe, typical of what happened across the United States. College professors joined their colleagues in the high schools in arguing effectively for the value of Latin study. Principals, superintendents, and school boards were constrained to listen, and often they were convinced. Success, however, was always contingent upon the cooperation of, and communication among, the friends of Latin in town, at school, and on campus. Programs were often lost at the critical moment when these three sources of support were not rallied and the realistic opportunity for success was ignored.

During these days of crisis in the late 1960s and early 1970s the most vulnerable moment in the life of even a thriving high-school Latin program was the time when the Latin teacher retired. During the years when Latin was under attack, teachers themselves, aided by the enthusiasm and devotion they personally inspired from their former students who held prominent positions in the community at large, were usually quite capable of squelching efforts to phase out their programs. Upon their retirement, however, they were honored and eulogized as irreplaceable, a statement, alas, taken literally by too many principals and superintendents.

In order to deal with this particular problem, at my own initiative as a Classics professor at the University of New Hampshire and secretary of the New Hampshire Classical Association (NHCA), I began to gather the names of persons interested and qualified to teach Latin. These names were published annually and distributed to all high-school administrations in our state. Now it could no longer be said that suitable people to teach Latin were unavailable to replace venerable retirees. At the same time, I also began to circulate to as many qualified classicists as I could essential information about Latin positions at schools whose Latin teachers had retired or were planning to do so. Principals and superintendents were not, it must be said, always delighted to receive, *volentes nolentes*, applications from competent and energetic classicists for posts they were not too anxious to fill.

In the academic year 1973-74, I published the names of 20

candidates: in 1974-75 there were 23, and in 1975-76, 36. Positions listed in those years numbered only 3, 6, and 6 (3 of them for Latin in combination with either English, French, or German), but in 1976-77, with 23 candidates registered, I was able to advertise 7 positions for full-time Latin and 11 combination positions.

In 1975 Professor Gilbert Lawall of the University of Massachusetts urged me to join him to extend across New England the services of what had become de facto a Latin Teacher Placement Service. He proposed that I continue to collect the names of candidates for Latin positions who from now on would come from all parts of the country and would be charged a modest fee to cover the operating costs of the Service. In addition to handling all correspondence with candidates, I would arrange their dossiers so that Professor Lawall could retype them on standard forms and send them out to school administrators with Latin positions open. Professor Lawall also volunteered to take over the task of locating Latin openings and compiling lists, which he then would mail to all of our registered candidates. The only remaining task, the management of the modest finances required to run the Placement Service, was to become the province ex officio of the NHCA Treasurer.

Notices of available teaching positions began to come from every region of the country, as well as from Canada and even Europe. The majority of these were combinations of Latin and some other subject (see Tab. 1). The number of candidates also grew, coming from more distant states, with many anxious to find

TABLE 1: Latin and Combination Positions Advertised, 1984-86.

	84-85	85-86
Teaching positions (total)	127	118
Teaching positions shared with CAAS	50	
Full-time Latin positions	43	64
Part-time Latin positions	18	
Latin—English positions	18	8
Latin—French	17	10
Latin—Spanish	12	10
Latin—German	2	3
Latin—Greek	3	1
Latin—Russian		1
Latin—French and/or Spanish	6	
Latin—History		2
Latin—Social Studies	2	
Latin—Mathematics	1	
Latin—other combinations	11	19*

*Latin and modern foreign languages

openings in New England schools. By the academic year 1978-79, our new Placement Service was functioning under the triple aegis of NHCA, CANE, and the Classical Association of the Atlantic States (CAAS). In 1978 it had registered 46 candidates and located 86 teaching positions; in the next year these figures jumped dramatically to 72 and 107, respectively.

By the early 1980s, since most, if not all, New England state classical associations were to one extent or another supporting the efforts of the Service, it took on appropriately its present designation, the New England Latin Placement Service. It may be added that the running of this Service requires constant, but not excessive work, the total of which is done on a *pro bono* or rather, more aptly, a *pro causa Latinae* basis, so that candidates continue today to be charged no more than the modest fee of $15 for its services.

As can be seen from Tables 2 and 3, the numbers of candidates have regularly increased in recent years as have also the variety of the candidates' qualifications. In recent years, too, the number of Latin jobs has continued to exceed the number of registered candidates: there were 84 candidates for 127 positions in 1984-85 and 97 candidates for 118 openings in 1985-86. The one vital statistic that has unfortunately been beyond our capacity to obtain is the precise follow-up of candidates' success in actually landing jobs. Certain conclusions, however, can be drawn. State certification, whether we like it or not, is usually essential for employment in the public secondary-school system, the source of about 90 of our available positions. The MAT degree, such as that offered in the graduate program at the University of Massachusetts (see Keitel, above, pp. 63-70), with multi-state certification, produces something of a triple-A candidate, in these days almost absolutely assured of employment. By contrast, the MA degree held by a great many of our candidates at times fails to impress high-school administrators who are anxious about "overqualification," as they often term it. The same negative must even more be stressed in evaluating the prospects of candidates with the PhD, 12 of whom registered with the Service in 1985-86.

Apart from the good ratio of exclusively Latin jobs (both full-time and part-time) to candidates exclusively qualified to teach Latin, there seems to be a generally good match of candidates and positions which call for such combinations of skills as Latin-English or Latin and a modern foreign language (see Tab. 1-2). What is surprising and, in my view, unfortunate is that, although many of our candidates are both interested in and

TABLE 2: Candidates and Their Areas of Competence, 1982-86

	82-83	83-84	84-85	85-86
Candidates overall	69	73	84	97
Candidates with state certification	29	36	56	46

Majors, minors, areas of competence (individual totals exceed total number of candidates, as some candidates had multiple areas of competence)

	82-83	83-84	84-85	85-86
Straight Latin/Greek/Classics	18	13	22	39
Latin—English	13	23	22	30
Latin—French	10	14	10	14
Latin—Spanish	9	8	7	5
Latin—German	1	7	5	8
Latin—Italian	1	2	1	1
Latin—Russian			1	
Latin—Japanese				1
Latin—Linguistics	1			
Latin—Comparative Literature	1	1	1	1
Latin—History	19	16	14	13
Latin—Social Studies	4	4	7	6
Latin—Political Science	1	1	1	1
Latin—Government	1			
Latin—American Studies		1		
Latin—Business Administration				1
Latin—Accounting				1
Latin—Economics	1		1	1
Latin—Education	3	1	3	1
Latin—Educational Administration				1
Latin—Botany		1		
Latin—Chemistry			1	
Latin—Mathematics	2		2	2
Latin—Computer Science	1			
Latin—Psychology		1	3	2
Latin—Philosophy		4	5	5
Latin—Art	1			1
Latin—Art/History		2		
Latin—Music		1	3	4
Latin—Theology	1		1	

TABLE 3: Final Degrees of Candidates, 1984-86

	84-85	85-86
MAT	16	16
MA	26	46
MED	1	1
MSED	1	1
JD	1	
"ABD"	1	1
PhD	7	12
BA, BS, etc.	31	18
Other		2

qualified to teach history, relatively few such high-school combinations have appeared among the positions listed by our Service.

While I would not want to exaggerate the role of the New England Latin Placement Service in the resurgence of Latin in the Northeast—so many factors have been important in this phenomenon here in New England and across the nation—it may nonetheless be allowed that the resurgence we are enjoying would not have been so steady nor so successful without this mechanism for identifying positions and candidates and facilitating communication between them. This service (and others like it, including, on the national level, that of the American Classical League: see Wilhelm, below, pp. 145-57) is but one example of the sort of voluntary collaboration on the part of school and college classicists that has been, and will remain, essential to the well-being and vitality of our profession.

For further information on the New England Latin Placement Service, or assistance in organizing a state or regional placement service, write

Professor Gilbert Lawall
71 Sand Hill Road
Amherst, MA 01002

Professor Richard V. Desrosiers
209-A Murkland Hall
University of New Hampshire
Durham, NH 03824

Assistance is also available from Professor Robert Wilhelm and from the other Latin Placement Directors whose names and addresses are provided in the following article and directory.

Latin/Greek Teacher Placement Services in the United States and Canada

Robert McKay Wilhelm
Miami University

The following catalog of national, regional, and state Latin/ Greek teacher placement services has been prepared with three purposes in mind: 1) to aid the high-school and elementary-school administrator who is seeking a Latin/Greek/Classics teacher; 2) to provide the prospective Latin/Greek/Classics teacher with a list of placement services through which a pre-college teaching position might be obtained; and 3) to put into the hands of Classics departments, colleges of education, and state foreign language consultants a comprehensive listing of placement services for teachers of Latin, Greek, and Classical Studies.

AMERICAN CLASSICAL LEAGUE (ACL) LATIN/GREEK TEACHER PLACEMENT SERVICE: The ACL is the only classical organization to provide a national placement service for announcing Latin, Greek, and Classical Studies positions for high-school and elementary teachers. To qualify for registration with the ACL Latin/Greek Teacher Placement Service, the registrant must 1) be a current ACL member (annual dues are $15) and 2) pay a registration fee of $10 per annum, September to August. The ACL Placement Service maintains a dossier on each registrant, consisting of an information form, three letters of recommendation, and a curriculum vitae. A monthly newsletter listing teaching positions is sent to all registrants; during periods of high job activity, the newsletter is mailed bi-weekly. Credentials are forwarded to prospective employers upon request from either the registrant or from the school administrator.

The information form which all registrants are required to complete requests the following information: 1) the type of position preferred (public high school, non-public high school, college, university, elementary, or junior high school); 2) geographical location preferred (New England, Mideast, Southeast, Great Lakes, Plains, Southwest, Rocky Mountains, Far West, specific states preferred); 3) certification qualifications and states where certified; 4) date available to assume a teaching position; and 5) permission to release registrant's name and telephone number to school administrators who call seeking candidates available to fill an immediate vacancy. For each registrant this information is maintained on computer so that when school administrators call the ACL office requesting "a teacher certified in Latin/French who wants to teach in the Southwest," we are able to do a computer search and provide immediately the names of possible candidates.

Job information is obtained through a variety of sources: 1) school administrators and state foreign language consultants send announcements about teaching positions to the Placement Service office (there is no charge to the school for advertising in the job newsletter); 2) retiring teachers inform the Service of the need for a replacement; 3) the regional and state placement services forward job information to the ACL Service; and 4) miscellaneous reports of possible openings are verified by telephone.

There are three regional placement services:

CLASSICAL ASSOCIATION OF THE ATLANTIC STATES (CAAS) LATIN PLACEMENT SERVICE (Delaware, District of Columbia, Maryland, New Jersey, New York, Pennsylvania): Registration with the Placement Service ($15 per annum) is open to all classicists regardless of CAAS membership. The Placement Service sends a copy of the candidate's registration form to any school which announces a teaching position and distributes monthly bulletins to candidates with the address and telephone numbers of the administrators seeking teachers. An annual survey of schools in the CAAS geographical area is undertaken by the Director in order to locate teaching positions.

CLASSICAL ASSOCIATION OF NEW ENGLAND (CANE) LATIN PLACEMENT SERVICE (Connecticut, Maine, Massachusetts, New Hampshire, Rhode Island, Vermont): Registrants ($15 per annum) in the CANE Latin Placement Service receive periodic bulletins of positions open in the schools for teachers of Latin, Greek, and Classical Studies, and of these subjects in combination with other subjects. Copies of brief resumes submitted by candidates are sent to those school administrators who notify the Service of available teaching positions. All secondary schools in New England (public, independent, and parochial) are canvassed each year for openings for Latin teachers, and members of all classical organizations in New England are invited to notify the Service of openings for teachers that come to their attention (see further Desrosiers, above, pp. 139-44).

CLASSICAL ASSOCIATION OF THE MIDDLE WEST AND SOUTH (CAMWS: Alabama, Arkansas, Colorado, Florida, Georgia, Illinois, Indiana, Iowa, Kansas, Kentucky, Louisiana, Michigan, Minnesota, Mississippi, Missouri, Nebraska, New Mexico, North Carolina, North Dakota, Ohio, Oklahoma, South Carolina, South Dakota, Tennessee, Texas, Utah, Virginia, West Virginia, Wisconsin, Wyoming; Manitoba and Ontario): The Chair of the CAMWS Committee for the Promotion of Latin serves as contact person for Latin, Greek, and Classical Studies positions through the 32 CAMWS states and provinces, informing the Director of the ACL Placement Service of any teaching positions that become available within the CAMWS geographical area. The CAMWS state and province Vice Presidents are encouraged to monitor the status of Latin and the availability of teaching positions within the individual states, to serve as placement liaisons themselves, and to forward job information to the Director of the ACL Placement Service.

Several state classical organizations maintain placement services that monitor the status of positions within their individual states. The function of the placement contact person varies from state to state: some actively seek out positions for teachers, others act as facilitators in trying to place teachers in specific teaching positions, and others maintain full placement services that send out candidates' dossiers to school administrators.

In order to insure the most effective placement process possible, the various state, regional, and national placement bureaus need to remain in close communication, and school administrators need to be made more aware of the services those bureaus provide. Readers are urged to cooperate in the placement effort by notifying the appropriate placement services of available positions and candidates and by photocopying and distributing the following directory to state and local school personnel officers and other administrators.

ACL DIRECTORY OF LATIN/GREEK TEACHER PLACE-MENT SERVICES FOR SECONDARY AND ELEMENTARY TEACHING POSITIONS IN PUBLIC AND PRIVATE SCHOOLS.

NATIONAL PLACEMENT SERVICE

The American Classical League Latin/Greek Teacher Placement Service

Director:
Robert M. Wilhelm
American Classical League
Miami University
Oxford, OH 45056
Telephone: 513-529-4116 (ACL Office)
513-529-3991 (Office in Classics Department)

REGIONAL PLACEMENT SERVICES

Classical Association of the Atlantic States
Latin Placement Service

Director:
John C. Traupman
Department of Classics
St. Joseph's University
Philadelphia, PA 19131
Telephone: 215-879-7579

Classical Association of the Middle West and South
Committee for the Promotion of Latin

Contact Person:
Kenneth Kitchell, Chair
CAMWS Committee for the Promotion of Latin
Department of Foreign Languages and Literature
Prescott Hall 222
Louisiana State University
Baton Rouge, LA 70803-5306
Telephone: 504-388-6616

Classical Association of New England Latin Placement Service

Co-Directors:
Gilbert Lawall
71 Sand Hill Rd.
Amherst, MA 01002
Telephone: 413-549-0390

Richard Desrosiers
Classics, 209-A Murkland Hall
University of New Hampshire
Durham, NH 03824
Telephone: 603-862-3132

STATE PLACEMENT SERVICES

Alabama
Latin Placement Service

Contact Person:
Nancy Worley
PO Box 162
New Hope, AL 35760

Arkansas Classical Association
Latin Placement Service

Contact Person:
Joan Carr
Department of Foreign Languages
Kimpel Hall 425
University of Arkansas
Fayetteville, AR 72701
Telephone: 501-575-2951

California Classical Association, Northern Section
Latin Placement Service

Contact Persons:
Richard L. Trapp
Department of Classics
San Francisco State
    University
San Francisco, CA 94132
Telephone: 415-469-2068

Mary Kay Gamel
Department of Classics
University of California
Santa Cruz, CA 95064
Telephone: 408-429-2381

Helen Moritz
Department of Classics
University of Santa Clara
Santa Clara, CA 95053
Telephone: 408-554-4375

David Traill
Department of Classics
University of California
Davis, CA 95616
Telephone: 916-752-1011

California Classical Association, Southern Section
Latin Placement Service

Contact Person:
Virginia Barrett
355 Coronado Ave., Apt. 4
Long Beach, CA 90814
Telephone: 213-937-5411 ext. 252 (office)
               213-434-6058 (home)

Colorado Classics Association
Latin Placement Service

Contact Persons:

Joy K. King
Department of Classics
Box 248
University of Colorado
Boulder, CO 80309
Telephone: 303-492-8165

Tamara Bauer
Overland High School
12400 E. Jewell Ave.
Aurora, CO 80012
Telephone: 303-696-3700

Classical Association of Florida
Latin Placement Service

Contact Persons:

Sheila K. Dickison
Department of Classics
ASB-3C
University of Florida
Gainesville, FL 32611
Telephone: 904-392-2075

Justin M. Glenn
Department of Classics
Florida State University
Tallahassee, FL 32306
Telephone: 904-644-4259

Georgia Classical Association
Latin Placement Service

Contact Person:

Richard A. LaFleur
Department of Classics
Park Hall
University of Georgia
Athens, GA 30602
Telephone: 404-542-9264

Idaho
Latin Placement Service

Contact Person:

Cecilia A. E. Luschnig
Department of Classical Studies
University of Idaho
Moscow, ID 83843
Telephone: 208-885-3958

Illinois Classical Conference
Latin Placement Service
Contact Persons:

LeaAnn Osburn
Barrington High School
616 West Main
Barrington, IL 60010
Telephone: 312-381-1400
ext. 227

Donald Hoffman
2110 North Oak Park Ave.
Chicago, IL 60635

Indiana Classical Conference
Latin Placement Service
Contact Person:

Bernard F. Barcio
Pompeiiana Inc.
6026 Indianola Ave.
Indianapolis, IN 46220
Telephone: 317-255-0589

Iowa
Latin Placement Service
Contact Person:

Jeffrey L. Buller
Department of Classical Studies
Loras College
Dubuque, IA 52004-0178
Telephone: 319-588-7725

Kansas
Latin Placement Service
Contact Person:

Oliver Philips
Department of Classics
University of Kansas
Wescoe Hall
Lawrence, KS 66045
Telephone: 913-864-3153

Kentucky Classical Association
Latin Placement Service
Contact Persons:

Jane E. Phillips
Department of Classics
University of Kentucky
Lexington, KY 40506-0027
Telephone: 606-257-4782

Mary Beth Hoffman
P.O. Box 848
Danville, KY 40422

Louisiana Classical Association
  Latin Placement Service

  Director:
    Kenneth Kitchell
    Department of Foreign Languages and Literature
    Prescott Hall 222
    Louisiana State University
    Baton Rouge, LA 70803-5306
    Telephone: 504-388-6616

Michigan Classical Association
  Latin Placement Service

  Contact Persons:
    Norma W. Goldman or Ernest J. Ament
    Department of Greek and Latin
    Wayne State University
    Detroit, MI 48202
    Telephone: 313-577-3032

Minnesota
  Latin Placement Service

  Contact Person:
    Stanley Iverson
    Department of Classics
    Concordia College
    Moorhead, MN 56560
    Telephone: 218-299-4155

Mississippi Classicist
  Latin Placement Service

  Contact Person:
    Robert Babcock
    Department of Foreign Languages
    Mississippi State University
    Mississippi State, MS 39762
    Telephone: 601-325-3480

Missouri Classical Association
  Latin Placement Service

  Contact Person:
    Kathy Elifrits
    HCR 32, Box 316
    Rolla, MO 65401

Nebraska
Latin Placement Service

Contact Persons:
Kathryn A. Thomas
Department of Classics
  and Modern Languages
Creighton University
Omaha, NE 68178
Telephone: 402-280-2637

Rita Ryan
111 South 49th Ave. #4
Omaha, NE 68132

New Mexico
Latin Placement Service

Contact Person:
Diana Robin
Department of Modern and Classical Studies
University of New Mexico
Albuquerque, NM 87131
Telephone: 505-275-9077

New Jersey Classical Association
Latin Placement Service

Contact Person:
Dorothy Lange
Rutgers Preparatory School
1345 Easton Ave.
Summerset, NJ 08813

New York (Classical Association of the Empire State)
Latin Placement Service

Contact Persons:
Joseph Heintzman
1600 Elmwood Ave. #3
Rochester, NY
Telephone: 716-461-0275

Richard Gascoyne
Associate Bureau of Foreign
  Language Education
New York State Education
  Department
Albany, NY 12234
Telephone: 518-474-5928

North Carolina Classical Association
Latin Placement Service

Contact Person:
Georgia Minyard
Department of Classical Civilization
243 McIver Building
University of North Carolina
Greensboro, NC 27412
Telephone: 919-379-5214

North Dakota
Latin Placement Service

Contact Person:
Carol Andreini
2800 8th St. #304
Fargo, ND 58102
Telephone: 701-280-1655

Ohio Classical Conference
Latin Placement Service

Contact Person:
Robert M. Wilhelm
Department of Classics
Miami University
Oxford, OH 45056
Telephone: 513-529-3991

Oklahoma
Latin Placement Service

Contact Person:
John S. Catlin
Department of Classics
University of Oklahoma
Norman, OK 73069
Telephone: 405-325-6921

Pennsylvania Classical Association
Latin Placement Service

Contact Person:
John C. Traupman
Department of Classics
St. Joseph's University
Philadelphia, PA 19131
Telephone: 215-879-7579

South Carolina Classical Association
    Latin Placement Service

    Contact Persons:
        Ward W. Briggs, Jr.   J. Frank Morris
        Department of Foreign   Department of Languages
            Languages and Literatures   College of Charleston
        University of South Carolina   Charleston, SC 29424
        Columbia, SC 29208   Telephone: 803-792-5713
        Telephone: 803-777-2765

South Dakota
    Latin Placement Service

    Contact Person:
        Brent Froberg
        Box 171, Department of Classics
        University of South Dakota
        Vermillion, SD 57069
        Telephone: 605-677-5468

Tennessee Classical Association
    Latin Placement Service

    Contact Persons:
        William S. Bonds   Harry Rutledge
        Classics Department   Department of Classics
        University of the South   University of Tennessee
        Sewanee, TN 37375   Knoxville, TN 37996
        Telephone: 615-598-5931   Telephone: 615-974-5383

Texas Classical Association
    Latin Placement Service

    Contact Person:
        Karl Galinsky
        Department of Classics
        Waggener 123
        University of Texas
        Austin, TX 78712
        Telephone: 512-471-5742

Utah
  Latin Placement Service

  Contact Person:
    John F. Hall
    Department of Humanities and Classics
    Brigham Young University
    Provo, UT 84602
    Telephone: 801-378-6246

Vermont Classical Language Association
  Latin Placement Service

  Contact Person:
    Diane Adler
    Foreign Language Consultant
    University of Vermont
    Burlington, VT 05405
    Telephone: 802-656-3196

Classical Association of Virginia
  Latin Placement Service

  Contact Persons:
    Jon D. Mikalson   Martha Abbott
    Department of Classics   Fairfax County Public
    New Cabell Hall   Schools
    University of Virginia   Donald Lacey Instructional
    Charlottesville, VA 22903   Center
    Telephone: 703-924-3008   3705 Crestdrine
                                    Annandale, VA 22003

West Virginia
  Latin Placement Service

  Contact Person:
    Charles O. Lloyd
    Department of Classical Studies
    Marshall University
    Huntington, WV 25701
    Telephone: 304-969-3166

Wisconsin
  Latin Placement Service

  Contact Person:
    William W. Kean
    Suring Public Schools
    P.O. Box 158
    Suring, WI 54174

Wyoming
Latin Placement Service

Contact Person:
Mark Mathern
1969 South Chestnut
Casper, WY 82601
Telephone: 307-234-6453

CANADA

Ontario
Latin Placement Service

Contact Person:
Ross S. Kilpatrick
Department of Classics
Queen's University
Kingston, Ontario
Canada K7L 3N6
Telephone: 613-547-3163

Manitoba
Latin Placement Service

Contact Person:
Rory B. Egan
Department of Classics
University of Manitoba
Winnipeg, Manitoba
Canada R3T 2N2
Telephone: 204-474-9502

Alberta
Latin Placement Service

Contact Person:
Barry Baldwin
Department of Classics
2500 University N.W.
University of Calgary
Calgary, Alberta
Canada T2N 1N4